Praise

"In reviewing *The Podiatry Practice Business Solution* by Dr. Peter Wishnie, one thing struck me: Why wasn't this book available when I started practice? Too often, books like this are based on theory or supposition. Dr. Wishnie is a practicing podiatrist who, whether in his practice or in those with whom he has consulted, has seen it all. You can hear his experience flowing off the page.

If you've ever heard Dr. Wishnie speak, you can picture him sitting next to you and carefully explaining the steps to take to improve your practice. I recommended this book for everyone in private practice, whether you're a new practitioner or a seasoned veteran, whether you're struggling or think everything is running perfectly. Everyone will benefit from reading this book."
– *Andrew Schneider, DPM*
   Vice President, American Academy of Podiatric Practice Management

"I've been in practice for more than forty years. Growing and developing a practice would have been much easier if I'd had a copy of Dr. Wishnie's book, *The Podiatry Practice Business Solution*. If I was asked to suggest the two best books on practice promotion and practice success, I'd recommend buying this book and reading it twice!"
– *Dr. Neil Baum*
   Professor of Urology, Tulane Medical School

"The absence of business skills often places physicians at a disadvantage as they evolve from the academic world to one that is fraught with challenges as private practitioners. *The Podiatry Practice Business Solution* captures, and then delivers, real-world solutions to many of those challenges. Whether you're a new or seasoned practitioner, you owe this book to yourself in order to make that evolution successful!"
– *John V. Guiliana, DPM, MS*
   Executive Vice President and Principle, NEMO Health

"Practical tips from a practice guru. Thirty years of experience generously shared! This book can literally change your life. Frustrated in private practice? Not sure where to start? Dr. Wishnie will guide you to your practice freedom. Success in private practice is still obtainable. Stop listening to the negativity and build your dreams!"
– *Marybeth Crane, DPM*
   Southlake, Texas

"After thirty years, just when I thought I knew everything there was to know about running a podiatry practice, along comes Peter Wishnie, and I feel like a rookie again. His combination of common sense, wisdom, humor, and experience shine through in what is the quintessential "how-to" guide to building a successful podiatry practice. Like a personal trainer for your practice, this book gives you the methods, outline, and accountability that will cause you to thrive—if you read it and follow the instructions. Thanks, Peter, for your tremendous contribution to our field."
– *Scott L. Schulman, DPM*
   Indiana Podiatry Group, Indianapolis, Indiana

"If you're looking for an intelligent and supportive guide to help grow your practice, there's no better person to lead and teach than my friend and colleague Dr. Peter Wishnie. His book is a top-to-bottom ready reference filled with expert advice, proven strategies, and easy-to-follow, practical steps for building a practice—and a life—you will love."
– *Dr. David Weiman, LPC*
   Weiman Consulting, Philadelphia, Pennsylvania

"I met Dr. Peter Wishnie in 2012 in Nashville, and I immediately knew that he viewed the business of podiatry differently than everyone else. Thank God he decided to share his experience and wisdom by writing this book. What Peter has shared is not just inspirational, it's also practical. If you follow his advice, your podiatry business can only GROW, and after you read it…read it a second time."
– *Tyson E Franklin*
   Author, Podiatrist, and Host of *Podiatry Legends Podcast*

"Whether you are a business owner, entrepreneur, or doctor, this book, *The Podiatry Practice Business Solution*, provides a clear roadmap for success in your life! I met Dr. Peter Wishnie while I was in residency and have been following his direction ever since. He is a true leader, coach, and friend."
– *Bradley Schaeffer, DPM*
   Podiatrist, Family Foot & Ankle Specialists

"Colleagues, this is the latest and greatest business of podiatric medicine guide from one of our best practice management gurus, Peter Wishnie, DPM. Peter provides an incredible look into the business of practicing podiatric medicine, reflecting on many years of successful practice. Dr. Wishnie is a proven and accomplished expert in the field of podiatric practice management, and this guide to running your BUSINESS as a business—while providing stellar medical care—is an absolute must read."
– *Michael King, DPM*
   Past President, APMA

"Managing any business is never easy, and each business has its own idiosyncrasies. Podiatry is no exception, and Peter Wishnie, DPM has written a management book focused exclusively on managing a podiatry practice. No longer do DPMs and their

teams have to learn from dentists, or chiropractors, or non-medical management books. Destined to become a classic in its field, *The Podiatry Practice Business Solution* belongs in every podiatry office. Get a copy for yourself and for every key person on your staff."
– *Rem Jackson*
  CEO, Top Practices

"If you're committed to building a successful private practice and want to minimize your risks and mistakes along the way, this is a must-have tool. Dr. Wishnie provides a detailed formula that outlines everything you need to know to build the practice of your dreams. I've had the honor of being coached by Dr. Wishnie, and I highly recommend any of his work. Your practice will prosper if you implement the information contained in this book!"
– *Tony Abbott, D.Ch.*
  Collingwood, Ontario, Canada

"This book offers a fresh, easy-to-read, straightforward approach to creating your successful life and business. Dr. Peter Wishnie shares key strategies to not only thrive in the medical field, but to also master the business side of the business. What impressed me most about Peter is that he does the work! He's a lifelong learner and has a heart to serve. Peter has walked the path and now generously shares his wisdom about how to run a successful practice while feeling fulfilled in all areas of your life. If you want more from your life and business, this book will inspire you and offer the plan that can help you have the life and business of your dreams."
– *Cathy J. Hanlin*
  C-Level Executive, Life Strategist and Results Coach

"Being a doctor should be fun, profitable, and enjoyable. This book is an illuminating guide and a pleasurable read, and it WILL help you run a practice that allows you to live your best life!"
– *Denise R. Bonnin, DPM*
  Family Foot & Ankle Specialists

"When it comes to building a successful/profitable practice that you'll love, Dr. Peter Wishnie knows what to do. Better yet, he's done it himself and he's an expert at not only what to do, but the elusive how to do it. I'm an attorney, but I'm no stranger to building professional practices, and Peter's simple and easy-to-understand process will help you get the joy back and have more of what you've always wanted, worked for, and deserved from your practice. Read this book, then do what he teaches."
– *David M. Frees III*
  Attorney, Adviser and Creator of The Business Black Ops Events and the Business Force Multiplier System

"Ever since I introduced Dr. Wishnie to advanced podiatric technologies in the late 1990s, he's proved to be a forward-thinking physician and leader. Initially, I was train-

ing him—showing him how to use technology like ESWT and therapeutic lasers. Since then, he has taught me lessons in leadership and management. Peter allows the people around him to make their ideas, goals, and dreams come true via specific management procedures. *The Podiatry Practice Business Solution* encompasses the best of his invaluable experience throughout an exemplary thirty-year career."
— *David Zuckerman, DPM*
Excellence Shock Wave Therapy, Zuckerman Future Technologies,
Medical Director/Podiatry Consultant

"Peter is the best of the best in his profession! What I love about Peter is that he's a student first and is always sharpening his sword to become better for his business and his family. I encourage you to dive into this book and, more importantly, to implement what he teaches you. Your business will go to the next level, just like you've been wanting it to!"
— *Bryan Dulaney*
Founder and CEO, Perfect Funnel System

"My medical practice has been successful but full of trial and error, especially in running the business side of things. I wish I'd had this excellent resource to help me when I started—and throughout my career. I'm glad Dr. Wishnie shared the struggles and obstacles that made his practice stronger and made him a better physician and business owner. Even if we think we do everything right, we'll have roadblocks and unexpected problems that can bring us down. This book is an invaluable guide to help you navigate those roadblocks. Thank you, Peter, for your wisdom, knowledge, and willingness to pass on such valuable and practical advice!"
— *Evan C. Merrill, DPM*
Medford, Oregon

"Dr. Peter Wishnie was the very first person who ever told me I could have my 'own' practice. Since our initial meeting in 2007 to today, I continue to consider Peter to be the expert in podiatric private practice management, a mentor to myself and hundreds of other physicians, and, most importantly, a great friend. This book encapsulates the essence of Peter's teaching and is THE recipe for your success. I cannot recommend it more!"
— *Dr. Melissa J. Lockwood*
Founder and CEO, Heartland Foot and Ankle Associates, Bloomington, Illinois

"I've known Dr Wishnie for many years and have been amazed at his ability to organize and manage a medical practice. He's a master at running the podiatry business and a master at helping others do the same. In writing this book, he's distilled his powerful formula for running a podiatry business and teaches you how to get back your nights and weekends. Learn his formula so you, too, can live your ideal life."
— *Brandt R. Gibson, DPM*
American Fork, Utah

"When I first met Peter, I thought I was at the top of my game with my podiatric practice. After interacting with him, I knew I had a lot of work to do. His knowledge in running an efficient, productive podiatry practice was far superior. With Peter's help, I was able to take my practice from good to GREAT—and beyond! The knowledge Peter conveys in his book can easily do the same for you."
– *Kevin S. Molan, DPM*
   Charlotte, North Carolina

"I am honored to be mentioned in Dr. Wishnie's book, and it was my pleasure to have been able to contribute to Peter's skill sets. Dr. Wishnie's book is a great read; it is to the point. Many of our colleagues go into practice but have no idea how to actually run the business or the back office. They may be great physicians, but they lack the skills to manage all aspects of the medical business. This book has great insights to prepare you, the physician, for being a better businessperson."
– *Bruce Werber, DPM, FACFAS*
   Scottsdale, Arizona

"If you've ever dreamed of owning your own medical practice, then *The Podiatry Practice Business Solution* is for you. If you've ever dreamed of being the respected CEO of a well-run, profitable, and successful business, then *The Podiatry Practice Business Solution* is for you. If you are just starting out in practice, or are nearing burnout, then this book is for you. In this must-have reference guide, Dr. Wishnie has created a roadmap using easy, actionable steps to help you not only survive, but thrive in today's independent practice environment."
– *Jenny Sanders, DPM*
   San Francisco, California

"Peter is one of the most genuine people on the planet. He is my friend, doctor, and client. I've known him for many years and am thrilled that he has finally written this book. The advice given in these pages will save any business owner years of frustration, doubt, shame, guilt, and debt. Peter knows his stuff."
– *Tom Foster*
   Founder and CEO, Foster Web Marketing

"I've known Peter for fifteen years, and I consider him to be one of the greatest authorities in leadership and coaching in our profession. This is especially true for this book that tells you everything you need to know to flourish in your podiatry practice. This is a must-read for new practitioners, associates, and experienced practitioners who want to navigate their future success. If you enjoy and love being a podiatrist and want to propel your business to new heights, there's no greater authority for practice management and coaching than Dr. Peter Wishnie."
– *Craig H. Thomajan, DPM, FACFAS, FAENS*
   Austin, Texas

"Dr. Peter Wishnie has written a must-read primer for anyone looking for a successful way to practice medicine and be a rock star CEO of their business. Read this book and learn from one of the best in the podiatry space."
– Stephanie Saliba
Former Employee and Continuous Mentee, Team Leader at Bloomberg

"From undergraduate school through the completion of a residency program, doctors spend at least eleven years in training. During that time, they typically amass $300,000 or more in student loan debt. Unfortunately, many of the problems doctors face in practice today are not only clinical problems, they are business problems—problems for which they are unprepared because they have received little to no business education. Dr. Wishnie suggests that it is equally important to invest in your business education. Fortunately, he's written this book, *The Podiatry Practice Business Solution*, which presents "everything you need to know to flourish in your podiatry business." This book will guide you toward the type of investments you need make in your business education."
– Jon A. Hultman, DPM, MBA, CVA
Author, *Reengineering the Medical Practice* and *The Medical Practitioner's Survival Handbook*

"Peter Wishnie has put together a sequential guide for anyone who wants to start, expand, and/or grow their practice or business. The ideas, concepts, and guidelines in this book have been applied and tested for success. Peter has personally applied these to his own practice. I highly recommend this book to anyone who desires success at the highest level, whether in business or in their personal life. A must read!"
– Vidya Sartorius
President, VMS Consultants, LLC.

"I've known Dr. Peter Wishnie for seven years and have had the honor to work with him as a Practice Management Leadership Consultant for four of those years. When Dr. Wishnie speaks, I make sure I listen. I've always learned something new and practical to apply to my life and our practice. He is a gifted teacher and a wise business-person."
– Tina Del Buono
Practice Management Performance Consultant

The
Podiatry
~~Practice~~
Business
Solution

The Podiatry ~~Practice~~ Business Solution

Everything You Need to Know to Flourish in Your Podiatry Business

Dr. Peter Wishnie

STONEBROOK PUBLISHING

Stonebrook Publishing
Saint Louis, Missouri

A STONEBROOK PUBLISHING BOOK
©2020 Peter Wishnie
This book was guided in development and
edited by Nancy L. Erickson, The Book Professor®
TheBookProfessor.com

Library of Congress Control Number: 2019918514

ISBN: 978-1-7339958-5-6

www.stonebrookpublishing.net
PRINTED IN THE UNITED STATES OF AMERICA
10   9   8   7   6   5   4   3   2   1

Dedication

This book is dedicated to my parents, Sy and Judy. I miss them very much, but the values they taught me are with me every day, particularly the value of persistence. They taught me that I could accomplish anything my heart desired with persistence. They didn't care if I became a doctor; they just told me to be the best at whatever I chose to become. Without the values of persistence and dedication, this book would have never been written.

I also dedicate this book to my three sons, Samuel, Alec, and Benjamin. As I was writing it, I wanted to inspire you and show you that no matter how old you are, you can make your dreams come true.

Contents

Foreword

You're about to embark on an exciting journey of growth, transformation, success, and fulfillment. Congratulations! I'm delighted for you because your guide on this journey is the most accomplished medical practice leader I've ever met. I recommend that you read this book straight through once, and then read it a second time and study it carefully. It will become one of your most valuable resources as you build your own well-run practice.

I first met Dr. Peter Wishnie in 2006, when I led a workshop in Columbus, Ohio on practice marketing and growth. About forty people attended that first meeting. At one point, I asked the group if they'd ever written down their goals. Three people raised their hands and said that they had. Peter said that he'd not only written them down, but that he carried them with him. Then he reached into his breast pocket and produced them in a nice holder. I could immediately tell that this man had his act together. What impressed me most, then and to this day, was that he didn't need to show off, he just wanted to learn. His lifelong-learner approach coupled with a true servant's heart is what makes Peter Wishnie so special.

After the workshop, he explained that he wanted to help other doctors enjoy their careers and make more money, and he wanted to teach like I had that day. I came to know him very well, and I learned how well he runs his practice. I was impressed to see how he and his excellent staff operate. It's all about systems and knowing their numbers. Peter is an avid student of other smart people, and he took good ideas and made them his own. Along the way, he invented quite a few of his own.

Top Practices began to offer professional development courses for doctors and their staff in 2010, and Peter led those courses that focused entirely on his systems and protocols. Now he's written a book that is destined to become a classic not only for medical practices, but for any professional practice or business.

I'm delighted that you've chosen to go on this journey with a guide who can show you the way to success. He's been my guide, partner, and friend as I've traveled on my own journey. Peter has inspired me and countless others, and I'm so thankful that we met all those years ago. He's a role model for his tenacity, his bias towards action, and his exceptional integrity.

Remember to not only read this book, but to implement what you learn right away, as Peter himself would, and then continue to build and refine. If you do, you'll enjoy your practice and your life more each and every day.

– Rem Jackson
CEO, Top Practices

Introduction

My journey to becoming a doctor started when I was nine years old. At first, I wanted to be a pediatrician, not a podiatrist. From the age of three until I was about fifteen, I was in and out of hospitals because of my asthma. I was a strange child in the sense that I liked going to the doctor. Not being able to breathe is very scary, and I remember my mother dragging me into New York City taxis to get to the doctor. When I asked her if I was going to get a shot, she'd say yes. Most children would have cried, but I was elated to get an injection. The magic elixir in that syringe would let me breathe again. To me, it was a miracle, and I wanted to be the doctor that helped other children one day.

As I progressed through my undergraduate studies at Stony Brook University in Long Island, I rethought my desire to become a pediatrician. Pediatricians have long hours and, at the time, they were one of the lowest paid of all physicians. I loved kids, but I knew that sometimes the parents would be too much to handle. I consulted my guidance counselor, and she suggested I look into podiatry. A family friend was our local podiatrist, and I went to his office to shadow him at work. He loved what he did, and it seemed like he had a good life. Podiatrists get to treat a lot of different problems, and since I get bored easily, I thought podiatry would fit my personality.

In 1983, I started my studies at the then California College of Podiatric Medicine in San Francisco, now known as The California School of Podiatric Medicine at Samuel Merritt University. I chose this school because it was known for its excellence in biomechanics. Plus, it had its own hospital and surgery suite. Back in 1987, not everyone got a surgical residency out of podiatry school, and the two schools that had the highest rate of residency acceptance was CCPM and a school in Philadelphia, now known as Temple University School of Podiatric Medicine.

San Francisco was absolutely amazing, but getting through my first year of podiatric school was one of the hardest things I've ever done. I'm glad I persevered. After I graduated and completed a one-year surgical residency, I was given the opportunity of a lifetime: I was accepted as the lone fellow in foot and ankle surgery at Hadassah Hospital in Jerusalem, Israel. It was one of the best years of my life.

I was trained by a different board-certified podiatrist every month. I learned so much from every one of those doctors, but I learned the most from Dr. Irvin Donick from Maryland and Dr. Bruce Werber, originally from Rhode Island. Dr. Donick had an incredible knack for teaching intra-operatively without ever taking the scalpel from me. He described what he wanted me to do, and his descriptions were so thorough that I was able to carry out his orders exactly. It's truly an art to teach someone verbally, where most attending physicians—including me—need to demonstrate the technique to students first. Dr. Donick told me that I was capable of opening my own practice, and I definitely took that to heart.

Dr. Werber honed my surgical skills. He had many little techniques that made the surgeries go a lot smoother. He also taught me how to think during the surgery, not to be robotic or to treat every case the same way. I am deeply grateful for the great training I received while in Israel because it gave me the confidence to open my own practice.

In December 1989, I purchased my practice in Piscataway, New Jersey. I remember that day very well. I walked in the front door, and my first patient was in the waiting room. Of course, he wondered who I was. I introduced myself as the new doctor and told him that I'd purchased the practice because the previous doctor had retired. He was a little cranky to say the least. He immediately pushed himself up on his cane and said, "I'm outta here." The funny thing is that it didn't bother me at all. I had a new practice and I knew I'd eventually grow it to become the best practice ever.

But I did have some doubts, and it wasn't smooth sailing at first. The first few months were tough. I couldn't keep my employees, I was losing an average of $7,500 a month, and I had bills to pay. Then I received a fax that said: *Do You Want to Learn How to Run Your Medical Practice?* It was like that old antiquated machine had been listening to my thoughts. That fax got my attention, and I paid $99 to attend a two-day seminar in New York City. I was definitely looking forward to learning something, so I was happy to take the bait.

After two days in the seminar and countless hours with the salesman, I pulled out two credit cards and paid the guy $18,000 for a year of coaching. Later that night, I stared at my bedroom ceiling and thought, *What the hell did I just do?* My practice was losing money, and I'd just maxed out two credit cards. But it ended up being one of the best decisions I'd ever made. At the end of my first year in practice, I'd made more money than the previous owner had made in any of his seventeen years, and I was in the black. I thought about how I'd spent so much money on my podiatry education but not enough to learn how to run a business. That's why I continually invest in my education. I never want to stop learning.

Whatever problem I face in life, I know I can find the solution at a local Barnes & Noble. If there's something troubling me, I go to that bookstore, grab a Starbucks, and do some research. Some people go shopping for therapy; I go to bookstores. It's cheaper and quicker than going to a therapist. This doesn't mean I'm against therapy, and I actually have a great life coach.

But when I wanted information about a business problem I needed to solve, I had to turn to books written by and for dentists, chiropractors, and even a urologist. There was not one good book for podiatrists. That's why I wrote this book—to give you a resource for running your business.

This book combines two of my great loves: business and books. Because I've read so many business and self-help books over the years, I want to share that knowledge with my fellow podiatrists. No one taught me how to run a business, and that may be the case for you, too. This book will teach you how to run your practice so that your practice doesn't run you.

I've been in private practice for more than thirty years. The best advice I can give you is to build the practice you want to have. Don't envy someone who has ten offices with thirty doctors, and don't make judgements about the doctor who has a small mom-and-pop shop. Bigger is not necessarily better. Live your dreams. Know what you want and then make it happen. Let me show you how.

CHAPTER 1:

No One Taught You How to Run a Business

"Build your own dreams, or someone else will hire you to build theirs."
– Farrah Gray

I bet that when you decided to become a doctor, you weren't thinking about running a business. The reason most doctors go to medical school is to help people with their physical and emotional ailments. Maybe you were like me and always wanted to own your own practice, but I guarantee that when you were studying anatomy and physiology—or when you were averaging three exams or practicals over a six-week period—you weren't thinking about how to make your private practice successful.

If you were like me, you may have taken only a brief, two-hour class on practice management. That was it. If you didn't pursue an MBA after medical school, then you had no idea how to be a businessperson, much less the CEO of your own practice. Most of us had to learn the hard way, by trial and error. And that can be very costly. The average medical student graduates with between $200,000 to $300,000 in debt. And if you take out a business loan on top of that, it puts a lot of pressure on you to produce immediately. When you start your own practice, there's no time for trial and error because erring can lead you down a very dark tunnel.

But don't get me wrong. You need to make mistakes because that's the only way to learn. The key is not to make any *catastrophic* mistakes.

I've never worked for anyone else, so I didn't learn how to run my medical practice by working under another doctor. I took courses and read many books on practice management and marketing, and I learned how to manage a profitable and thriving practice by learning from all kinds of specialists, including chiropractors and dentists.

To be successful in life, you must be a constant learner. It doesn't matter what your profession is; things simply change, and you need to stay on top of the new rules, new tools, and the new best thing.

Being an owner isn't for everyone. There are advantages of working for bigger corporations—the main one being that you're simply a doctor with no staff worries, no financial headaches, and no stress over all the government regulations. You can go to work, help your patients, and go home. But—and to me this is a big but—you're an *employee*. You have to do what your employer tells you to do. You have specific hours, a certain number of vacation days, and you take home a defined salary.

I believe that private practice in the United States is alive and well and will continue to thrive. In this country, people get to decide what they want, and when it comes to medicine, they still want individual, one-on-one care. Most people go to a preferred doctor, and they want to see that doctor every time. They don't want to spend time in the waiting room, and they want to get better fast without extra costs. If you can provide the best service, patients will come to you instead of anyone else.

This book is for the doctors who want the autonomy of running their own practice and want to learn how to do it.

This book is for the doctors who want the autonomy of running their own practice and want to learn how to do it. It will help you succeed in the business world and show you how to get your nights and weekends back.

There's no reason for you to spend crazy hours in your office. Being successful means that you're successful in all areas of your life, including your relationships, your family, your health, and just having fun.

:::::

Owning and running a private medical practice is no easy task. You're actually running a business, and it's full of challenges and pitfalls that your medical training didn't prepare you to handle. After all, you went to school to become a doctor and to treat patients, not to master skills like hiring, collecting the money you're owed, and training your staff. Yet, in order to be the CEO of your own practice, you must have those skills to lead a successful and profitable practice.

So, what's it like when the average physician starts a private practice? How do so many doctors end up burned out, exhausted, frustrated, and yearning for other options? Take a look at this hypothetical life cycle of a doctor:

1. You spend four years as an undergraduate, go to four years of medical school, finish an internship, and complete a three- to six-year residency program. During this twelve- to fifteen-year educational period, you work hard and know that, one day, you'll be licensed to practice medicine.

2. After that, you go to work for someone else. It's rare, especially today, that a doctor opens his or her own practice straight out of residency. While working for someone else, you work hard, work late, and do all the things you need to do to make a living and earn the respect of the practice owner.

3. Eventually, you may become a partner in that practice or move on to own your own private practice. No one wants to be an associate forever. To achieve the financial freedom you want, you need to run your own show. You want to be the "Big Kahuna."

4. After launching out on you own, you realize that it will take two to three years to make a profit. Now you work more than ever, but it's okay— you're putting in the time now to reap the rewards later. You *have to* work this hard to pay the rent and the staff salaries.

5. Then things tend to ease up. You have a nice flow of patients, and you're making more money. You start to feel good. Maybe you buy the house of your dreams. Maybe you take that expensive vacation.

But things start to change. Expenses pile up. It becomes increasingly challenging and tedious to comply with regulations. New technologies or other services become the "must haves" in private practice, and you wonder if you really need them to stay competitive. Over time, you get burned out. You realize that, if you take off time from you practice, the money will stop. Now you spend more and longer hours in the office, not just for a once-in-a-while occurrence. You're now a slave to your own practice.

How about you—do you still work weekends? Do you go home for dinner, or are you stuck at the office? Do you ever sit down and think about what life would be like if you had more control over your own time? Could your practice work with or without you to oversee it all? Could you take off three months to travel?

If you don't have control over your own life and think that your practice *can't* operate without you, then this book is for you. You'll learn systems to help you work *on* your practice instead of working *in* the practice. You'll learn how to put your office on autopilot and watch it run like a smooth, well-oiled machine. Your practice will transform into a turnkey operation. You'll find solutions to gain control and know how to set up these systems, which offer predictability in your practice. You'll know exactly how to generate the cash to give you the lifestyle you want. What you're building is freedom: the freedom to do whatever you want, whenever you want.

> What you're building is freedom: the freedom
> to do whatever you want, whenever you want.

What dreams have you pushed aside because you didn't know how to achieve them? Write them down, because this book will bring you new hope, a new vision, and a new surge of confidence.

The Early Days

When I purchased my practice for $100,000 in 1989, I was twenty-nine years old. I was also in debt for $100,000 in student loans, plus I had to take out a $100,000 line of credit for the capital needed to run the practice. At the time, I thought I'd purchased a pretty decent practice, but I later found out that the previous owner had discharged most of his patients because he was afraid this young "whipper snapper" was going discover the truth about all his botched surgeries. As it turned out, he'd been sued three times over the last several years. When I took over, I was barely seeing thirty patients a week—and definitely not bringing in enough money to pay the bills and live a decent life.

To increase my patient base, I purchased a mailing list—something you would definitely not do today because nobody reads mail anymore. I stayed up until midnight every night for weeks stuffing letters and sending them to the list. This helped a little, but it didn't make much of a dent in the bottom line. But I had confidence in myself as a doctor and a positive mindset. I simply focused on making my practice better and looking for ways to attract more patients.

Then one day, I received the fax I told you about in the Introduction. What a huge risk to take with all that debt! I was nervous, but hopeful. I promised myself to be a good student and do whatever they told me, as long as it was legal and ethical. And it was the best decision I'd ever made. After my first year in practice, I netted six figures.

Doctors spend hundreds of thousands of dollars for medical education, but then we're afraid to spend anything to learn about business or have a consultant coach us. Spending money on further education is an investment in your business, and if you don't know how to be the CEO of your practice, you need to learn.

But if you try to teach yourself everything, it can be very costly and time consuming. That's why you need to get a coach; it's the same reason why I have a personal trainer. I already know how to do all the exercises, but I don't know if I'm doing the right exercises to achieve my goals. That's how my trainer helps me. Further, doing the wrong exercises the wrong way could hurt me—just like running your practice improperly could cause pain in your pocket.

If you don't know how to run your business efficiently and effectively, you'll work crazy hours to make ends meet. Working harder but not smarter eventually leads to burnout. Even if you get home at a decent hour, you may be so preoccupied with the burdens of your practice that you're not present when you're there. You don't feel like playing with your children or reading them a book, and if you do, you fall asleep in the middle of it. You'll dread going to work every morning. You'll drag yourself out of bed and have a scowl on your face when you enter the office. Your staff won't be happy and, of course, they'll constantly come to you with problems. You'll wonder where the patients are and why you have so much downtime. On top of that, your husband or wife will want to take a vacation, but you can't afford to take time away from the practice—plus you don't have enough money to go anywhere. You're grumpy when you go home, you're useless to your family, and you argue with them over little things.

A poorly run practice can make your life miserable. The solution is to learn how to run it effectively and efficiently.

A poorly run practice can make your life miserable. The solution is to learn how to run it effectively and efficiently.

When you're an associate, your income is always limited. So, if you're going to work hard and sacrifice, you ought to do it for yourself and control how much money you can make. The fundamental reason you own your practice is to be in control of your time and money. Of course, you didn't mind putting in long hours at first, as long as it paid off in the end. Now you need to learn how to make it fun and profitable.

CHAPTER 2:
Your Recipe for Success

"It is literally true that you can succeed best and quickest by helping others to succeed." – Napoleon Hill

Doctors love recipes. We go to school and learn to ask patients specific questions, so we can get a complete picture of their symptoms and problems. We perform the proper diagnostic tests, and after that, we can determine a differential diagnosis. If a patient experiences the symptoms of A and, upon clinical examination, we see and feel B, then the patient has C, which is the diagnosis. It's comparable to an investigation.

I've learned to treat my practice the same way. If the money isn't coming in, I have to figure out why. When did this begin? What happened? Who was involved? As the CEO of my practice, I don't sit around doing nothing, hoping that things will change. Instead, I gather the troops and investigate the cause of the money leak.

How would you like to have a blueprint for the recipe for sustained success? Wouldn't it be great to look for your practice's symptoms and find your diagnosis? It sounds simple, and it really is. The problem lies in the fact that doctors are so busy that we don't have time to think. We're moving way too fast, but we can only speed up if we truly slow down. That's what you'll do on your rainmaker day, the day you analyze your practice and work on your SWOT—your strengths, weaknesses, opportunities, and threats.

Before discovering this recipe, doctors didn't know how to run their practices with intent. It was more of a fly-by-the seat-of-your-pants scenario. There were no systems or protocols in place. Everyone in the practice did things their own way, and nothing was consistent.

Imagine going to McDonald's and getting a hamburger that was cooked differently each time, or instead of getting your order in a few minutes, it took half an hour. McDonald's would never have been successful if they hadn't implemented systems that they replicated in every location.

For your practice to achieve the maximum success, you must not only have systems, but good people to implement them.

For your practice to achieve the maximum success, you must not only have systems, but good people to implement them. Of course, this is more serious than cooking hamburgers because you're treating people. Your staff members must be able to think. I look for people who are outgoing and friendly and can think on their feet—traits that cannot be taught. You don't necessarily need a boisterous person, but you definitely want someone who is happy and is usually smiling.

Ingredient #1

The first ingredient in your recipe for sustained success is *your vision*. It may be hard to see what you want your practice to be like in ten, fifteen, or twenty years, but you probably know what you want it to be like *now*. Extend that out three to five years. Better yet, think about what your practice would need to look like to give you an amazing life!

Your practice exists for one reason only: *to give you the lifestyle you so deserve*. It's there to give you a great life. To some, that means providing for your children, or going on trips with your significant other, or having a boat you can take out at night and look at the beautiful sunset with a glass of wine in hand. You need a reason, a purpose to work so hard.

Certainly, there will be times when you go home at the end of the day and feel like you didn't achieve much, or you saw thirty to forty patients that day and feel you have nothing to show for it. What will keep you going is your purpose and vision.

To be successful, you need a vision for your amazing life. Write down what a perfect day would look like. What time do you get up and what would you do? How do you feel as you enter your office? What's the mood amongst your staff? How do the patients feel before, during, and after your care? Include other things in your vision, like what people say about your practice, the size of your organization, how much you work, what kind of patients you see, and how many vacations you take per year. Write it all down.

The truth is that you can manifest whatever you want. And you can have more good days than not if you visualize precisely what you want in your life. Visualize how you'll handle certain situations so you can achieve the outcome you want. For example, let's say you need to discuss a staff member's poor performance. Instead of flying by the seat of your pants and saying things you shouldn't, visualize the conversation and think about what you plan to say. Picture how you'll respond to any negative reactions he or she may have.

Write down your vision, and read it to yourself daily. Allow it to sink into your subconscious mind. Your subconscious mind is constantly searching for the things you desire. If you're looking for a specific house or car and you can easily visualize and describe it, you'll find it because your subconscious mind was looking for it, even if you weren't thinking about it at that very moment. That's why it's so important to know exactly what you want. On the flip side, if you're confused and don't know what you want from your practice and your life, your subconscious mind will also be confused, and it can't help you.

Share your vision with your staff, but with this warning: don't explode your vision all over them. Lead your people to embrace your vision by asking them questions. Ask them about their vision for the practice. Ask them how they want to be treated when they go to a doctor's office or a fancy restaurant. Probe them for the nitty-gritty details that span from the time when they call for a reservation to finishing their meal and leaving for the night. Then incorporate their answers with your vision. Have an open discussion and, together, write down this new vision. You'll find that their vision won't be much different from yours.

Ingredient #2

The next ingredient in your recipe for sustained success is your mission statement, which is slightly different from your vision. Your vision describes what your practice looks like, and your mission is what you do, why you do it, who you are doing it for, and what you represent.

For example, Ben & Jerry's Ice Cream has three separate mission statements—social, product, and economic. Their product mission is "to make, distribute and sell the finest quality ice cream and euphoric concoctions with a continued commitment to incorporating wholesome, natural ingredients and promoting business practices that respect the Earth and the Environment." This is a beautiful mission because it distinctly describes what kind of product they produce and how they're different from other ice cream makers; they make ice cream while respecting the earth and the environment.

Our mission at Family Foot & Ankle Specialists is to SERVE, which is to provide great *WOW!* Service to our patients and anyone who walks through our doors; to provide Excellent care to our patients; to Restore the patient's foot and ankle function; to be Visionaries in the foot, ankle, and healthcare industries; and to Educate our patients and staff in foot and ankle care.

Family Foot & Ankle Specialists
"Consider yourself one of the family"

Mission Statement

Our mission is to **SERVE**:

Stress free environment for our patients. This is a place where people come in and feel comfortable with the doctors and staff, knowing that we have their best interests at heart. It is a stress-free workplace for the staff, where they know they are appreciated and respected.

Excellence in foot and ankle care. Our doctors are experienced and trained to handle all conditions of the foot and ankle. We provide a wide range of treatments for numerous ailments, according to what best suits the patient's needs. The staff at Family Foot & Ankle Specialists excels in their work and can handle any other patient needs, from financial to physical.

Restoration of foot and ankle function as quickly as possible is our goal. We understand the world is moving at a very fast pace, and it's our job to get you back on your feet quickly. We understand that you need to maintain total health and to keep up with the speed of life.

Vision: At Family Foot & Ankle Specialists, we strive to keep up to date on the latest techniques and technology. Our vision is to grow with the needs of our patients and be the best of the best.

Educated doctors, staff, and patients. Our doctors and staff are continually educated through seminars and workshops. We also actively educate the public and our patients about proper foot and ankle care and the abilities of a podiatric physician.

You may think that sounds great, but how would you incorporate your mission statement into your daily practice? When one of my staff members has a question about what to do in a certain situation, I ask them, "What do you think we should do?" This empowers them to make great decisions according to our mission, plus it proves that I not only talk about our mission, but I live and breathe it every day.

This empowers them to make great decisions according to our mission, plus it proves that I not only talk about our mission, but I live and breathe it every day.

Here's an example. Sometimes a patient returns an item like a walking boot when they found one cheaper online, or they already had one at home, or any other reason for the return. But when you see the boot, it's obvious that they've walked miles in it. In fact, the boot is worn out and can't be reused. You can either argue with the patient (customer) and say you can't refund their money, or you can reference the mission statement, which is to give *WOW!* customer service, and simply say, "No problem. We can do that for you." Which scenario would create a better outcome? And by the way, how much did that boot really cost the company? Is it worth arguing over and losing a patient who might've referred their family and friends? Even worse, do you want to risk having them posting a bad online review?

Every person on your staff must buy into your mission. When they all understand and embrace it, they're less likely to say, "Hey, I'm not doing this. It's not my job." When it's everyone's responsibility to SERVE the patients, then they're all responsible to provide a wonderful experience. In essence, your mission statement unites the staff so they can start working as a team.

Talk about your mission statement during your weekly meetings. Get the staff involved and ask them if they want to add anything to it. Ask if the statement motivates them to make decisions and to do a better job. Then don't put it aside and forget about it—and don't let them forget about it either! Bring it up in your morning huddles, and use it to help each person make daily decisions.

Ingredient #3

The third ingredient in your recipe for sustained success is your purpose statement. Your purpose statement tells why you do something and why you exist. In my practice, our purpose is not to help people with their foot and ankle conditions, but this: *we give people their lives back by helping them get back on their feet.* This means we care about the total patient, not only about their foot pain. How is the patient limited by their foot and ankle problem? What can't they do because of the pain? This is why we're in business. This is our purpose.

What's your purpose? Why are you in business? What makes you excited to go to work every day? You might say, "I'm at the point of giving up," or, "I don't really care anymore because no matter how nice I am or how much time I spend with my patients, I don't feel appreciated. And on top of that, I work my butt off and the reimbursements are so damn low." I get it, and I definitely have moments like that myself. That, my friend, is why you need a purpose.

> **When you review your vision, mission, and purpose—not only for your practice, but for your life—then you can get in the right mindset to make your work meaningful.**

When you review your vision, mission, and purpose—not only for your practice, but for your life—then you can get in the right mindset to make your work meaningful. Your subconscious mind will activate and start thinking of ways to make your dreams come true.

Here's a tip: be positive! If you're negative, you can't possibly think of solutions to your problems. Only a positive mind allows you to be open to new ideas and new solutions. The way to do this is to *slow down*. If you're disgruntled about your practice or your life, you may stop caring and start operating without intention.

> **Only a positive mind allows you to be open to new ideas and new solutions. The way to do this is to slow down.**

It's important to live intentionally, so take time to sit down and ask yourself some really good questions like, "How can I solve this problem quickly and inexpensively? Who do I know who's been through this same situation and came out of it on top?" A confused mind can never come up with solutions. Carve out time to sit down, reflect, and think—and be sure to schedule that time for yourself. If it's not on your schedule, it won't get done. So, set aside a couple of hours of uninterrupted time and lock your door. Turn off your phone, close your email and anything else that pops up or dings. Better yet, get out of your office and go somewhere else for your think time.

Ingredient #4

The fourth ingredient in your recipe for sustained success is to create sustainable, repeatable systems. This means you'll need to compile a comprehensive operating manual. Having repeatable systems is what made McDonald's successful. Ray Kroc handed his operating manual to each franchise owner and told them, "Here's your recipe for success. Just follow the operating procedures, and your bank account will be sizzling like the hamburgers you are making." If they didn't follow the systems, they were fined. That's how important systems are.

Have you ever hired a good and experienced employee, then found out that they didn't do their job the way you wanted them to do it? But how could you expect them to do it your way if you never trained them? This is why your operating and procedural manual is critical. In it, every job description is fully documented with the details about how to accomplish everything. When you hire someone new, you hand them the manual. There's no more guessing because it's all written down. But you can't just hand them a huge manual. They must be trained, and the manual is their guide.

Everything, *everything*, must be documented in your procedures manual: how to answer the phones, how to answer the many questions patients ask, how to schedule an appointment, how to schedule surgery, how to set up for surgical procedures, the list of supplies the medical assistant needs for each procedure, and even a section on medical terminology. Compile a manual for each position—one for the front desk receptionist, one for the medical assistant, one for the financial department, etc. I've even documented a job description manual for the cleaning crew that says, "Don't forget to dust the top of the pictures in the office." Call me crazy, but a dirty office can cost you a patient.

Without systems, you'll have chaos. People will make things up as they go along, and I guarantee you won't like it. If they schedule patients whenever they feel like it, you can be overbooked or have too much gap time between patients. The only way to have a smooth-running practice where you leave on time at the end of the day is to develop and enforce systems. Your systems are your roadmaps to success.

> The only way to have a smooth-running practice
> where you leave on time at the end of the day
> is to develop and enforce systems.

Having systems also allows for continuity of care. There should never be a case when one patient gets one thing and another patient gets something else. If these patients ever meet up (which isn't unusual since you have a referral-based business), they'll wonder why they were treated differently. In a practice with multiple doctors, your systems ensure that when one doctor is absent, the fill-in doctor follows the protocol to give the patient comparable treatment. The care is consistent, and the patient is happy.

Implementing systems will increase your bottom line. When you and your team follow all the protocols, your patients will get everything they need to feel better today. You'll speed up the flow because your medical assistants will have all the materials and equipment ready for you when you enter the room.

If you have an established office but no systems, it will, of course, take time to document everything you do in the practice. But doing so will add value to the practice, especially when it comes time to sell it. Here's a trick to document your systems in a very simple manner. Since each staff member is already doing their job, ask each of them write down—in detail—the steps to fulfill their job responsibilities. Give them about two months to complete this, then reward them with two additional paid days off or whatever else will motivate them to get the job done. Then all that's left is to edit the manuals.

I remember a few times when my numbers were down. Patient visits, production, and collections were dipping. At first, it was for only a few days, but then those days turned into weeks. I was going crazy trying to figure out why. But then I remembered that all I had to do was review my systems to figure out what we'd skipped.

For example, after a new patient visit, our doctors call them the next day to see how they're doing and to ask if they have any additional questions. Every new patient also gets a thank you letter from us, which restates their medical problem and the treatment plan. Further, we send a report of our findings to their primary doctor. This seems so simple, but it's something special we do to differentiate ourselves from other doctors. It also fulfills our mission statement to educate our patients about their foot and ankle conditions. When these steps aren't followed, patient referrals go down, which will increase the chance that the patient will skip their next appointment. This small step creates a domino effect that impacts charges, collections, visits, and new patients.

I found out that our numbers were dipping because we'd neglected to make the calls and send out the letters. So, we plugged that hole and the numbers went up again.

If your systems are working for you and if you adhere to them, it's like baking a cake. You bake the same chocolate cake over and over and everyone raves about it. But one day your cake is terrible. What happened? Perhaps you ran out of an ingredient, or you eliminated something, or you made a substitution. These small diversions make a big difference. If your system is working well, don't change anything about it. Following your documented processes matters.

Next, you can review your processes to tighten things up. When you see a downward trend, a tweak or two is all that's usually required. Review the flow chart of your systems and assess each area to discover the bottlenecks. With the help of your team, you can immediately unblock the bottlenecks and realize a quick upward trend.

Here's an example. Let's say there's a line of patients waiting to check out. The phones are also ringing, and other patients want to check in. Other than having a crowd around the reception desk, what other effect does this long line have? If these patients waited to get into the treatment room, then waited for the doctor to come in, and are now are waiting to leave, there's a good chance they're irritated, and there's an even greater chance they won't show up for their next appointment. There could be several reasons for the bottleneck: not enough front desk staff, the patients ask a lot of questions about costs, there's a lot of chitchat between the staff member and the patients, or the patients need to check their calendar to make their next appointment.

You address the problem at a staff meeting and decide to change the procedure for making follow-up appointments. From now on, follow-up appointments will be made in the treatment rooms instead of at the front desk. You'll also make sure the patient's benefits are close at hand so they know their financial responsibility before they check out. Just a few simple tweaks in the system can put you back on the road to success.

More to the Recipe

Systems and protocols are critical, but there's more to the recipe for success. Consider establishing distinct departments in your practice, kind of like a grocery store. You know how stores are organized; they're laid out according to departments, and within each department are separate aisles. The grocer knows that the cake ingredients are in aisle five, and the milk and butter are in the refrigerated section in the back. And if the shopper organizes their grocery list by aisle, then the shopping experience is simple. The same is true for your office. Divide your practice into departments and assess each department separately so you can make a plan for each one of them. Then the head of each department will know what he or she needs to accomplish.

Here are my department suggestions:

1. **Executive Department:** This is you, the doctor. You're responsible for all final decisions.

2. **Personnel Department:** This is usually the office administrator, and he or she is the one in charge of hiring, firing, and training. The doctor-owner is also involved and has the final say in hiring and firing decisions.

3. **Marketing/Public Relations Department:** If you have a marketing director, then that person is responsible for this department. In some offices, the doctor likes to take charge, but the busier you get, the more difficult it becomes.

   Many practices don't focus on marketing, but that's a mistake. You can't grow without marketing. This book isn't about marketing, but I offer a couple of ideas that will help you grow your practice. If you want or need guidance to market your practice, I recommend that you visit www.toppractices.com. Rem Jackson, the CEO of the company, offers many ways to help you grow your business.

   In the meantime, write down all your marketing ideas and figure out how to implement them immediately. If you don't have anyone to implement your ideas, then hire someone, maybe just part time—like a college student who is studying marketing. Eventually you'll need a full-time marketer.

4. **Production Department:** This team includes everyone who produces, such as the doctors and medical assistants. *Producing* means anything that increases your bottom line. The doctor-owner is usually in charge of this department, but if you have a lead medical assistant, then he/she can also play a big part in managing this area.

5. **Financial Department:** Do you handle your billing in house or do you have a billing service? If you outsource your billing, make sure you have access to all your information and reports whenever you want them. If you can't sleep because something's bothering you and you want to investigate, your data must be accessible and you need to be able to run the reports yourself. If you can't do that, you need to find another billing

company—or at least figure out how to access that information any time you want it. You should never be held hostage for *your* information.

6. **Quality Control Department:** Every business needs a quality control department. When things go wrong, how are they handled? You'll learn how to delegate 95 percent of these issues, but sometimes you have to get involved. When a patient calls about their bill and the financial team has tried their best to handle it but the patient is still upset and gets angry, what happens next? Do you sweep it under the rug, or do you jump on the phone to handle it yourself? You can't afford to ignore anyone. It leaves a bad taste in the patient's mouth, and they'll feel like you don't care. Simply calling the patient might be enough.

Quality control also involves simple but important things, like keeping the bathroom clean. Patients could easily think that if the bathroom isn't clean, your instruments might not be either. Of course, you won't be cleaning the bathroom yourself (but it should not be beneath you, and if you do clean the bathroom once in a while, it will show great leadership) but don't ever ignore it. Ask a staff member to please clean it, and then ask them why you should have to ask. The problem can easily be resolved by making a cleaning schedule, so you know who is responsible. Find out who's in charge of making sure this is done and hold them accountable.

The diagram on page 19 shows the purpose for each department. For example, your receptionist, who is in the Personnel Department—also known as the patient care coordinator (PCC)—has a purpose. He/she collects money at the time of service, collects past due balances, makes appointments, and makes sure the patients keep their appointments. His/her purpose is to keep the appointment book full of *productive* patients. Productive patients have billable services rendered to them. Follow-up visits and quick check-ups are examples of non-productive patients. Of course, you'll always take care of these patients, but you don't want a full day—or even a full hour—of non-productive patients.

Now that you know the responsibilities of this position, you can measure each one. Part of the PCC's job is to provide you a weekly report with graphs that show the percentage of kept appointments, the total weekly visits, and the amount of money collected. These numbers will tell you a story and will help you stay on track to reaching your goals. This is further discussed in chapter 8.

This is your recipe for success. Have a vision, create a mission statement, write down the purpose of your practice, and include protocols and systems. Further, surround yourself with the right people and make them responsible for what happens in their department. Your practice will never succeed if your staff members are lazy, don't care, or if they simply suck the life out of you, so make them accountable. You're the CEO of your practice, and your practice is here to give you the life you so deserve. Get rid of the people who aren't part of your vision for a great practice.

EXECUTIVE DIVISION

1. A viable expanding solvent organization with fully satisfied employees.
2. Business that is completely legally compliant.

PERSONNEL DIVISION

1. Effective personnel posted and trained
2. Communication easily accepted and delivered
3. Productive staff members

MARKETING DIVISION

1. Income greater than outgo plus reserves
2. Practice flooded with new and existing patients who refer others
3. New patients calling who are interested in our services

FINANCE DIVISION

1. Preserved and valuable assets and reserves
2. Collect all monies owed to the practice and keep accurate records
3. Maintaining accurate financial records and paying bills on time

PRODUCTION DIVISION

Patients who are 100% satisfied with their treatment, who return to the office and refer others.

Patient Care Coordinator:
1. Fully booked schedule of productive patients who are courteously greeted and keep their appointment.
2. Collect all monies owed at the time of service.

Medical Assistant:
1. Patients who are seen on time are comfortable, at ease, and are ready for treatment.
2. A fully equipped room available for the doctor to get the procedure completed smoothly.

Podiatrist:
1. Patients who are 100% satisfied with their treatment who return to the office and refer others.

QUALITY DIVISION

1. Effectively trained staff who obtains quality products in their divisions.
2. Number of dissatisfied customers discovered.
3. Dissatisfied handled to flawless service.
4. A smooth-running, flawless organization.

CHAPTER 3:

Getting Organized

"For every minute spent organizing, an hour is earned."
– Benjamin Franklin

Organization—oh, how many of us hate that word! Organization is not only important for your practice, but for your life. Making lists is certainly part of getting organized, but if you're constantly making lists and not completing the tasks, that's procrastination. In order to allow new ideas to flow, you have to remove the clutter from your life. And you can't focus on everything at the same time. So you must prioritize.

One of my problems is that I want to get everything done, and I want to get it done now. I can sometimes accelerate the pace by hiring people or delegating tasks. But at other times I need to slow down and think about the *one thing* that needs to be done that—if I completed it—most of the other things would fall in place.

For example, my practice was getting really busy and I needed another medical assistant, but it takes time to hire and train a new team member. I also knew that without another person, we couldn't keep up the pace and keep both the patients and staff happy. My medical assistants were all over the place, running around like chickens with their heads cut off. No one was having fun.

Finally, I called a time-out. I gathered my assistants and said, "I know the office is crazy and we'll figure this out, but right now we need to take good care of the patients who are here. I'll do my part to do whatever it takes. I'll bring my patients back to the treatment room myself, and I'll clean the rooms if I have to because our number one priority is our patients and providing them with exceptional service."

I reminded each team member about their primary focus and expressed that we needed to work as a team and help each other out however possible. The next day my office manager and I reworked the staff schedule. Thankfully, we had already cross-trained almost everyone. Then my office manager published an ad for a new assistant and, in the meantime, she worked the front desk.

:: ::

As your office grows, organizing its departments becomes increasingly vital to your success.

As presented in the last chapter, you must first list all the job responsibilities for each staff member, so they know what's expected of them. For every job, the first priority is: "Be a team player. Do whatever it takes to help your co-workers and our patients." This should eliminate what no employer wants to hear: "That's not my job."

Your office manager will use the lists to train new staff members. It's also a helpful checkpoint to determine how knowledgeable the staff is in respect to their job duties, and it can be a good reference during job reviews.

The next step is to create a mind map. A mind map is an organizational chart that shows the relationship of one department to another (see diagram below). Revisit the perfect recipe for success from chapter 2. Mentally walk through your office and think about how you want your patients to feel as they move through the different areas of your office.

Now take it further and document the process for every single step a patient goes through during his or her appointment. For example, the patient's first experience is the initial phone call. How will your receptionist answer the phone? What questions should he/she ask? What process does he/she follow to make an appointment? Do you reserve a specific day to see certain types of patients? The entire process should be thoroughly documented.

Next, document the process for when the patient enters the office; how they're escorted into the treatment room; when the doctor enters the room; the treatment process; and, finally, the checkout process. What actions do you and your staff need to take to make the patient's experience positive and memorable? If you want your patients to have an amazing experience, you must plan for it and then educate and train your staff to deliver what you envision.

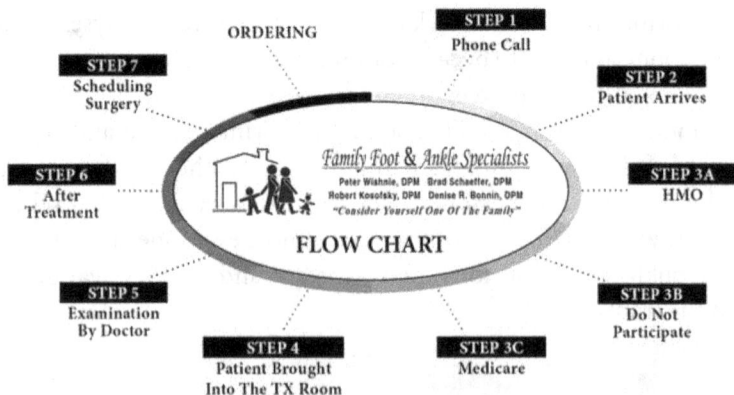

ORDERING

STEP 1
Phone Call

STEP 7
Scheduling
Surgery

STEP 2
Patient Arrives

Family Foot & Ankle Specialists
Peter Wishnie, DPM Brad Schaeffer, DPM
Robert Kosofsky, DPM Denise R. Bonnin, DPM
"Consider Yourself One Of The Family"

STEP 6
After
Treatment

STEP 3A
HMO

FLOW CHART

STEP 5
Examination
By Doctor

STEP 3B
Do Not
Participate

STEP 4
Patient Brought
Into The TX Room

STEP 3C
Medicare

You can also use your department mind maps as a tool to improve your practice because you can see at a glance which areas are excelling and which need to improve. When your office is organized, you provide your staff a stress-free working environment. Further, you give yourself a blueprint for successful growth.

It would be a huge mistake to grow your organization without organization. Adding additional offices or staff to an already chaotic scene is a recipe for disaster.

Even if your staff is well trained, your practice can still be disorganized. Things only work well when your staff operates as a team and communicate properly with one another. I'm sure you've experienced busy times where one staff member tries to be a superhuman but fails to communicate with his or her co-workers. They want to believe they're indispensable and can do it all. However, the end result is that they're all over the place and everyone's running behind. If this kind of thing happens in your practice, address it is during a staff meeting.

By now, you've already scheduled weekly meetings where everyone feels comfortable to discuss what's on their minds. Use these meetings to talk about what's going right and to give people a pat on the back. We call this giving *zaps*. Each staff member zaps another one for something they did to help them personally or to help the overall office. *Zap* is a powerful word that, when you say it, it sounds like what it represents—the feeling of electricity. We zap someone to electrify them, to make them feel good.

You should also discuss the chaos that occurred at the front desk (or whatever the current issue is) and get staff feedback. Your people might be reluctant to say that they can't handle the load with the current staff alone because they're concerned that you'll think they can't handle their job. No one likes to admit they can't do something, especially the really good people. However, you can review the mind map that has all the job descriptions to see if any steps in the processes were missed.

Even though you're a doctor and are busy seeing patients, you have to keep your eyes and ears open to know what's going on at the front desk. Walk around your office periodically. The goal isn't to find out what's wrong or who's messing up. That's far from your purpose. You don't want to micromanage. You want to know what's going *right*, so you can immediately compliment that team member. Whenever you see things that can be improved upon, make a note and bring it up at your next staff meeting.

If you think that's the office manager's job, you're both right and wrong. You're right in the sense that the office manager is more available than you are, and these tasks are in his or her job description, but wrong in another sense because the office manager doesn't own the practice. You need to see for yourself what's going on. Apple CEO Tim Cook makes surprise visits to individual Apple stores. Donald Trump used to make surprise visits to his hotels. He's a real neat freak and would go crazy if he saw any lint or dirt on the floor of his hotels. By the way, I'm speaking of the *hotelier* Donald Trump, not the *political* Donald Trump, so please don't misinterpret anything here. The point is that no matter how much money you have or how big you are, you need to check the pulse of your organization.

The point is that no matter how much money you have or how big you are, you need to check the pulse of your organization.

Your mind maps will also show the downstream effects that leaving out or ignoring a process has on other departments. Here's an example. Your patient is at the checkout area and pays the $50 co-pay in cash, but your receptionist fails to issue a receipt. She also fails to record the cash transaction in the patient's account. Thirty days go by and your financial department sends the patient a bill. The patient calls and says that she paid it in cash. What do you do? You could argue with her, but you might lose a patient over $50. And because you didn't keep track of her payment, she probably thinks your office is disorganized, so she won't refer anyone to you. You still might lose her as a patient because of the disorganization.

::::

Poor communication can be a big problem in a medical office. You can only have a well-run, efficient practice if you have excellent communication systems. In many practices, there are too many times when doctors get interrupted because the staff walks around, finds the doctor, and gives him or her a message. What a waste of time!

Verbal communication is the worst way to communicate because it interrupts established procedures and invites misunderstanding. In my office, I don't allow verbal orders—from the staff to the doctors or from the doctors to the staff. Your staff is doing many things and they need to focus on the matter at hand. Just like you, they don't want to be disturbed when they're in the middle of something. For the doctor, disturbances mean you'll lose your train of thought and could forget to prescribe a medication or forget to do something you promised the patient you'd do.

My associate doctors used to haphazardly tell the medical assistants what they needed. I witnessed this once. My associate saw a medical assistant come out of a treatment room to get something for the patient. He interrupted her to rattle off three things he needed from her. The assistant said, "Okay." I immediately stopped the interaction, and in front of the doctor, I asked her to repeat back what the doctor had asked her to do. She could only remember one thing. And it wasn't her fault. The doctor had interrupted her process.

So how do you communicate what you want from a medical assistant? Try using a combination of a flag system and a board or just post-it notes. Here's how it works. You need the assistant to go to room three. In my office, I have a system with lights and chimes. I press the appropriate button which means I need an assistant to come to the room I'm in. I put a post-it note on the chart holder outside the door that says exactly what I need her to do. I've also seen offices that have a whiteboard and the doctor writes what they want on the board. Then the doctor is free to go to another treatment room. Of course, this takes time, but believe me, it's faster and more efficient than relying on the assistant to remember what to do. This system definitely prevents mistakes from happening.

Establish several types of communication systems in your office, such as:

- **Communication boxes:** These are pigeonhole boxes, one for each staff member that has their name on it. Any mail or forms that need to be signed go in these boxes. The staff must handle them as soon as they can. The communication boxes should be near the front desk since that's where the mail is sorted.

- **Triages:** This should be part of your EHR system. Any messages regarding patient care should be sent to you by triage. Your EHR should be set up to tell you if the patient is requesting a refill on a medication. In addition, you should make every effort for your patient to use the patient portal system to retrieve their lab results, your notes, or to make a request.

- **Intra-office email:** In my office we use an app called Slack which allows us to message other staff members. We can also set up groups, like the medical assistant group, or the front desk group. If you have a message that pertains to multiple people, you send one message and everyone in that group receives it.

You also need a system for your staff to issue requests. You can create a form where they write down their request, the situation, and the solution.

Request: I need to take next Wednesday off to take my grandmother to the doctor.

Situation: The doctor is only available during this specific time.

Solution: I spoke with Mary and she will cover for me.

What does this accomplish? It shows that the staff member is taking responsibility for her job and has arranged for her own coverage—not you or the office manager. Both she and the person who's covering for her both sign and the date the form, and the office manager signs off on it.

Here's another example. Let's say a staff member's computer is extremely slow. She needs a new laptop because it's seven years old, and its slow speed is affecting her performance. She takes the initiative to research a new laptop and writes up the form.

Request: I need a new laptop

Situation: My computer is old and slow and is affecting my work.

Solution: I researched three different laptops and have attached three different purchase orders with pictures of each laptop. Here's why I recommended laptop B.

Again, this shows that the staff member has taken the lead to make the office more efficient. She didn't complain that she needs a new computer. Instead, she did all the legwork, possibly saving hours of your time.

:::::

In order to be efficient and increase productivity, you need organizational systems that help you clear your mind—something you can easily follow that prevents you from forgetting anything important. What system do you have for ordering lab work, orthotics, and shoes? How do you know if the lab has received your request or lost your prescription?

The number one reason why businesses fail is due to slow service. In today's world, we want and expect everything immediately. You can get almost anything you want within twenty-four hours. Amazon Prime has spoiled us, and so have our phones and computers. What that means to your practice is that if someone has to wait weeks for the orthotics you ordered for them and they're suffering in pain, they might not come back to you or write you a rave review.

That's why I recommend that you maintain an Excel spreadsheet to track everything you order. You can have a tab for orthotics, one for blood work, one for radiology testing such as MRIs and CT scans, and one for shoes. Every time you order any of these items, your staff will track it. They'll record the order date, the patient's name, and the item ordered. When the order arrives, the front desk person will open the spreadsheet and record the item's arrival. Store the spreadsheet on your server, so everyone in the office can access it.

Twice a week, someone should check the spreadsheet to see which items have arrived and which have not. If there are any delays, your staff should call the lab to find out why. Then—and this is where you differentiate your business from everyone else's—you call the patient and explain why the product or test results are delayed and let them know that you're on top of this. That, my friend, is *WOW!* service. To be the best, you have to do what others won't.

The purpose of being organized is to make sure you have a well-run, smoothly oiled machine—a practice in which everyone knows what to do and how to do it; a staff that communicates and works well together. You can only accomplish this if all your systems and protocols are written down. This is your office manual, the bible your staff will check when they aren't sure what to do when you're not around. The goal is to have your office function in an optimum fashion even when you're not there.

The goal is to have your office function in an optimum fashion even when you're not there.

Time Constraints

The main obstacle to documenting systems and protocols is that doctors say they don't have time to do it. Lack of time is never an excuse. If something's truly important, you'll make the time to do it. There are many books about time management, but I'll skip ahead and tell you that the first thing you need to purchase is a planner. Not all planners are created equally. Some planners are simply books where you write down to-do lists. That's not what you want. You need a planner that works for all of your goals. Not just business goals, but your personal, financial, health, and fun goals.

Now that you have your planner, carve out a day where you work on your practice, not in your practice. You're a business owner, and you must make time to wear the CEO hat. I call this day your rainmaker day. It's a day to write up your systems and procedures, as well as to work on your marketing and your finances.

I call this day your rainmaker day. It's a day to write up your systems and procedures, as well as to work on your marketing and your finances.

You won't be the only one working on your procedures. As a matter of fact, you may not work on them at all. Get your staff to do it! When I bought my practice, the first thing I did was write down all my systems and procedures. I recorded how I wanted my phones to be answered, how to set up for an ingrown toenail procedure, and just about everything someone would need to do. I wrote it myself because I had the time, plus everyone—including me—was brand new. But if you have an established practice and you're seeing patients all the time, there's no way you can do this yourself. Hopefully, you have key staff in each department. They should be the ones to write down their own job descriptions in full detail.

Your organizational systems must include the following:

Telephone Scenarios—If your phones aren't being answered properly, there's an excellent chance that you're losing money. Your phone represents the first impression you make on the patient. No matter what the patient asks, your staff always needs to answer the question with another question, which is, "May I have your name, please?" The most beautiful sound for a person is the sound of his own's name. Use their name throughout the conversation. This builds rapport and makes the patient comfortable.

Your phone procedures help your office to be organized. With good phone procedures, you'll decrease the patient's waiting time because you get their information, such as their insurance and demographic information, over the phone. You need written phone scenarios for the following:
- How to answer the phone
- How to make a new patient appointment
- How to reschedule patients
- How to handle cancellations
- How much an office visit costs

Scheduling Surgery—After the doctor discusses the recommended surgery with the patient and they agree to the procedure, you need a system to schedule the surgery. For example, the patient goes to the front desk with the encounter form that reads "discuss surgery." Your staff member then asks the patient when he or she would like to have the surgery and will give them a few open dates. They then schedule a thirty-minute appointment to discuss the surgery, where the doctor explains the procedure in full, informs them of all the possible complications, and discusses alternatives to the procedure. This is a key appointment because if problems arise later, no attorney can accuse you of rushing the patient to sign a consent form five minutes before going under anesthesia. Send the consent form home with the patient so they can read it as many times as they'd like. This gives them the opportunity to call you with questions or concerns prior to the procedure. If for some reason the patient gets scared and cancels the procedure, that's okay because they clearly aren't mentally prepared to have surgery. Of course, you'll want to call the patient if this happens because they might have misunderstood what you said or what was written, and you can set things straight.

The staff member who schedules the surgery should have a list of associated actions that must be performed (see table next page). This includes what needs to be done prior to and after the surgery, including pre-admission testing, verifying benefits, and confirming the time and date of surgery with the hospital.

It's important to make lists—lists that are easy to follow, that simplify the tasks for your staff, and that prevent them from being overwhelmed. If the person who schedules surgery has other duties, such as being the receptionist, then he/she must have a designated time to perform the scheduling duties. Otherwise, she'll make mistakes because she's trying to multi-task. Multi-tasking never works. And if she gets interrupted during her duties, the checklist will help her get back in the groove a lot faster.

It's important to make lists—lists that are easy
to follow, that simplify the tasks for your staff,
and that prevent them from being overwhelmed.

Because we can't totally eliminate interruptions, in my office, we use a three-bin system. The first bin is the to-do bin, the second bin is for things that were started but not completed, and the third bin is for things completed that need to be filed.

Unorganized people start a task, then move on to the next one before they complete the first. If you can't complete something right now, then don't start it. For example, if you open your mail, and you know it's going to require you to act on something but you don't have time to do it right now, don't open it yet. It's a waste of time and creates stress if you open it, set it aside, keep looking at it, and still don't have time do anything about it.

And don't allow your people to do this, either. It leads to a lot of mistakes and incomplete work. I've told my staff that their brain is like a computer; if too many files are open, the computer slows down. For that reason, they're instructed to complete the task they're working on before they start something new.

Of course, there will be times where they can't immediately complete a

TASK	COMPLETED	INITIAL	DATE
Surgery Checklist			
☐ Receive triage from Dr. to schedule			
☐ Ask patient for two possible dates			
☐ Schedule discuss surgery			
Booking Surgery			
☐ Verify patient benefits			
☐ Fill out minimum estimate sheet			
☐ Schedule surgery with facility			
☐ Enter surgery date in EMR			
☐ Call patient to tell them surgery date			
☐ Schedule post-op date after surgery			
☐ Put together surgery chart			
☐ Include directions to facility			
☐ Include consent form			
☐ Include pre- and post-op instructions			
☐ Include facility's paperwork			
☐ Include doctor's cell phone number			
☐ Contact any reps for the case			
At "Discussion Surgery" Appointment			
☐ Patient signs necessary forms			
☐ Give patient minimum estimate owed sheet			
☐ Does not sign consent form			
☐ Collect at least half of minimum owed			
☐ Copy consent form			
☐ Give patient the original			
☐ Patient signs on day of surgery			
☐ Chart goes in doctor's bin			
☐ Verify that patient made post-op appointment			
Prior to Surgery			
☐ Fax all parts to facility			
☐ Confirm surgery date and time			
☐ Get faxed facility confirmation			
☐ Medical clearance from MD			

task, such as when a patient calls to ask for copies of their records or when a patient needs someone to fill out their disability papers in the midst of a busy day. If someone else in the office can't fulfill these requests, then that staff member must put this request on a list as an action item to be completed by the promised date. It can usually be done on the computer because a lot of EHR systems allow you to make to-do lists.

Inventory Systems—This is a huge, because how you handle your inventory affects your bottom line. A lot of offices have either too little or too much inventory. Having too little is costly because you won't have the products to sell, plus you're not optimizing your patients' care. Having too much means you've stocked a certain item for more than forty-five days, and your capital is literally being stored in a closet instead of being used for something else, such as marketing or paying an outstanding bill. Designate a specific person to take inventory every week or two.

...how you handle your inventory affects your bottom line.

In my practice, we order supplies every two weeks. See our order form on page 32. Each order form is for a specific vendor. The staff member writes the vendor's name at the top and lists every item he/she will purchase from that company. She writes down the number of items she's ordering, the number of items already in stock, and the date of the last ordered. Look at the purchase order form.

For example, let's say we're ordering walking boots, and the last time we ordered was two months ago. We have six boots in stock and ordered twelve last time. The staff member wants to order another twelve boots. But why? In two months, we've only used six walking boots—three per month. Since we already have six, we'll be good for another two months. In this case, I wouldn't approve the order and would suggest we revisit the situation in two weeks. This is how we keep our inventory under control.

After the purchase order has been approved, a copy of it goes to the bookkeeper. I maintain a separate bank account for supplies, and this is when I move the total amount of the purchase order from our operating account to the supply account, which ensures that when I get the bill for the supplies, the funds are available. Unless there's an emergency, the money in the supplies account can't be used for anything else.

In a busy practice, it's the little things that can get left out, like checking the bathrooms several times a day for cleanliness, and inspecting the fire

Date: _____

From: _____

Co: _____

Family Foot & Ankle Specialists
Peter Wishnie, DPM   Brad Schaeffer, DPM
Robert Kosofsky, DPM   Denise R. Bonnin, DPM
"Consider Yourself One Of The Family"

REQ DATE	REQ BY	ITEMS TO BE PURCHASED	QUANTITY	COST TO SHIP	# IN STOCK	LAST ORDERED

Total Cost:

Supervisor's Approval: _____   Date: _____

Dr. Wishnie's Approval: _____   Date: _____

*Payment for any item(s) ordered without approval will be the responsibility of the employee who ordered it.

extinguishers, the oxygen tank, and the eyewash station, to name a few. Establish systems to stay organized and designate a person to be in charge of each one of them.

A well-organized office is better for you, your staff, and especially your patients.

CHAPTER 4:

Hiring Your "A" Team

"When you hire people that are smarter than you are, you prove that you are smarter than they are." – R. H. Grant

Your "A" team—this is what sets you apart from every other doctor's office. You can be the best damn doctor in the world, you can be funny, maybe do a little song and dance for your patients, but if your staff is horrible and rude, your patients will go somewhere else.

Hiring the right staff is critical. Remember that the patient is coming to you for the whole experience, not just your expertise. They're in pain, they're sick, and they don't want to be in your office. They're afraid of what you might say or do. Everyone on your "A" team must cater to them.

You've probably heard about inferior physicians who have amazing practices. It's because the staff and the doctor have an excellent bedside manner. The first rule of hiring is to hire for *personality*, not *experience*. I've had many great staff members who were very efficient. They dotted their i's and crossed their t's, but when it came to social skills, forget about it. They didn't last long.

In central New Jersey in the year 2000, an influx of HMOs and PPOs came our way, and patients now had to get a referral from their primary care physicians in order to see a specialist. Before this change, the patient could simply make an appointment, come in, and be treated. The new requirement meant that our office protocols had to change. For example, what would we do if a patient came in without the referral? Would we see them? Could we ask their primary doctor to backdate a referral, or did we have to turn away a person who was in pain? Further, we had to know which insurance companies required that patients get a referral. Even worse, these insurance companies reimbursed us at a lower rate. I had the same staff, the same—or even increased—overhead, and now received a lower reimbursement.

Prior to this, my staff was very efficient, and they followed the phone scenarios I put in place, which never asked the patient about what insurance they had. But I noticed that when the insurance game changed, my staff did too. They were so worried about getting the information correct that all their pleasantries went out the window. No more, "Hi, Mary, how are you? Glad to see you." It was more like, "Please sign in, and do you have your referral? Oh, you don't? Then we can't see you today."

Ugh! That's not what I wanted, and it's not what my practice is about. No matter what the government tells me I have to do, my patients come first. Period. I had a serious meeting with my staff, and I explained what I wanted them to do and how they should interact with our patients. But no matter what I said, they didn't change. So, I changed them. I fired three people on the spot. Adios. Take your bad attitude with you.

Here's something I've learned over the years: hire slowly, fire quickly. One bad apple can definitely ruin the bunch, and in this case, the bunch was bad. In 2000, I purchased an EMR system, got rid of my paper and file cabinets, let go of the high school girl that pasted the transcribed notes in each patient's chart (she was sweet, but no need for her anymore), relieved the transcriptionist of her duties, hired two new front desk people and a different medical assistant.

Here's my point: no matter what happens to medicine in the good 'ol USA, the patient experience will rule. Americans still insist on the right to choose—in everything. We go to the supermarket and have ten different choices for canned corn and a million choices for cereal. The patient will always have a choice of which doctor they want to see. Of course, patients with more disposable income have more choices, but that's true whether you're talking about doctors or buying a suit.

If you and a doctor down the street accept the same insurances, which doctor's office will the patient choose? They'll choose the one where they feel most comfortable.

If you and a doctor down the street accept the same insurances, which doctor's office will the patient choose? They'll choose the one where they feel most comfortable. It will be the office that shows that they really care about *them*, not their insurance.

Today, people look at online reviews for recommendations. If a friend or another doctor recommends your practice for foot and ankle care, the first thing the person will do is look at your website and your online reviews. And while they're searching for your practice, if they find another doctor that's close to them but has many more great reviews, you can bet that they'll go to that doctor. You just lost them to your competitor.

This is why hiring your "A" team—the team with great personality and social skills—is critically important. Hire slowly. Don't get desperate because you're in a bind and are short-handed. Yes, having one less staff member puts pressure on everyone else to pick up the slack and do more work. But the staff doesn't usually mind if the employee you fired was a bad apple. They were already doing double duty because that person didn't pull his/her weight or simply had a bad attitude. It only hurts when the employee left on her own accord and was a really good worker.

That's why I am a big proponent of having a bench. In sports, you have your starting team and then you have your bench. These are the guys or gals who literally come off the bench to give the stars a rest or to replace an injured teammate. If your office requires two front staff people and two assistants, then get a fifth person who can be cross-trained. Inevitably, one of your staff members will get ill, go on vacation, quit, or get fired. Then what? You're down a team member and must fill the void.

Even if your practice doesn't warrant having a fifth player, hire one anyway. There are so many things this person can do to add value. For example, they can check order statuses, they can help with marketing, they can answer the phone, and they can even do recall calls—phone calls to patients you haven't seen in a while to check if they need any further services. Even if you're paying this extra person $15 to $20 an hour, doing these odd jobs will give you a huge return on investment. He or she will probably even help you be more efficient and allow you to see more patients.

The Three-Interview Process

I use a three-interview process for each prospective employee. But before we dive into interviews, we follow a preliminary process. When we post the job opportunity, we know who we're looking for. I write down the essential requirements the new hire must have, and I don't settle for anything less.

Next, we review the resumes, which can give you a clue about the person. I look for inconsistencies, such as a lag in employment. What happened? Did the person go back to school, start a family, or what? I also look to see how often and how quickly they've changed jobs or careers. It's a big red flag if someone changes jobs every one or two years. If I see any misspellings or poor grammar, the resume immediately goes into the trash.

I don't always look for experience, because I can train and teach any position. What I can't train for is personality. Sometimes a person who has experience can be set in his/her ways and will do the job how he wants to, not the way I want them to do it. So, I prefer to train the right person for the job. For the front desk position, it's a bonus if the person has insurance experience because insurances are very complicated and are the hardest part to teach.

Having certain skills is non-negotiable, such as basic computer skills, the ability to read, and basic math skills. Why math? It's surprising how many people can't figure out what 20 percent of $100 is. If the patient is on Medicare and doesn't have a secondary insurance, and Medicare allows $100 for this particular service and will pay 80 percent, the staff member needs to figure out what the patient owes. They have to know how to calculate the patient's 20 percent.

We actually test for these skills during the interview process.

Interview 1:

After reviewing resumes, my office manager calls the good candidates for a preliminary phone interview and to explain the hours and the details of the job. If it's not a good fit, she moves on. She knows that our new hire must be bubbly and positive. I can't be around negative people, especially at work, where I spend about a third of my life.

Now it's time to interview. You can certainly be fooled during the interview. The prospective star can be on time and happy and can have a great smile. Anyone can fake it, but can they fake it consistently? That's why we conduct three interviews.

The first interview is with my administrator, the second is with me, and then they'll come back again to spend time with the staff. If they're late for any of these interviews, they don't get the job.

The administrator gets to know the applicant and determines if he/she would be a good fit for our organization. My administrator will probe to discover if the candidate can be cross-trained to optimize the office flow. She will discuss the hours of the job and ask if the candidate has any problems going to both of our offices. She'll also find out if the applicant has another part-time job. You want your employees to be fully dedicated to the job, versus having another night job they'll have to run to. The administrator will ask about the applicant's previous jobs and her specific duties. Other questions include the following:

- How long have you been looking for a job?
- Why do you want to leave your present job?
- How do you define customer service?
- Give an example of exceptional customer service you have received.
- How do you rate your ability to work in a fast-paced environment?
- How do you rate your organizational skills?

My administrator knows the pulse of the team, and we definitely do not want to disrupt the camaraderie we've developed, so it's critical that she understand if the applicant would be a good personality fit. We want our new hire to be professional and responsible and a strong team player. The interview can indicate some of these things, but it's even better to check their references.

> My administrator knows the pulse of the team, and we definitely do not want to disrupt the camaraderie we've developed, so it's critical that she understand if the applicant would be a good personality fit.

Interview 2:

The second interview is with me. I use a series of interview questions, which I learned from the book *Smart Hiring: The Complete Guide to Finding and Hiring the Best Employees* by Robert W. Wendover.

Interview Questions:

1. Why did you apply for this position?

2. What do you know about our company?

3. What do you know about podiatry?

4. What did you love about your old job?

5. What didn't you love about your old jobs?

6. What one thing did you do that you thought was difficult, but you tackled that task and did a great job?

7. Why did you leave each job and what did you do between jobs?

8. If I met your best friend, what would he/she say about you?

9. What motivates you?

10. Where do you see yourself in three and five years?

11. If you could have dinner with anyone, dead or alive, who would it be with and why? (This is just a fun question and breaks the ice in the middle of the interview. It can also tell you more about the person.)

12. What's important to you in life?

13. What makes you happy? Are you a happy person? (Listen for their tone and determine if they're truly happy or are just paying it lip service.)

14. What gets you upset?

15. Have you ever not gotten along with a co-worker or supervisor? Tell me about that.

16. What is your definition of a leader? How does a leader lead?

17. What is your definition of success?

18. Are there any obstacles in your life that could prevent you from being successful?

19. If there were two things you could change in your last or present job, what would they be and how would you change them?

20. How do you organize yourself for day-to-day activities?

21. What have you done to become more effective in your position?

22. Describe the best boss you ever had.

23. Do you like being in charge?

24. Have you ever been in charge of a department or project?

25. How would you provide a *WOW!* patient experience?

26. How would you handle a patient who is upset?

27. Think of a crisis situation where things got out of control. Why did it happen and what was your role?

28. What concerns should I have about hiring you?

29. What do you do if things are slow at work?

30. What are your hobbies?

31. Do you like to read? (Leaders are readers and I'm looking for future leaders.)

32. Role play: If they're interviewing for a front desk job, explain a scenario where they would have to collect a large sum of money. For example, the patient doesn't have insurance and it's their job to collect $500 for a pair of orthotics. You want to see whether this candidate can ask for money without assuming the patient can't afford it.

    The candidate should be a little tough. If she says, "Would you like to pay for that today?" in the back of my mind I'm thinking, *Would you— future employee—like to be paid on payday?* Their best comment would be, "The cost for today's services is $500. We take cash, check, and all major credit cards. How would you like to pay that *today*?"

    Many people have financial problems, so they assume that other people do, too. They might assume that $500 is a lot of money for the patient. You can't have people like this in your money stream. They must be committed to collecting the amount due at the time of service.

33. Another item I role play with is the "I want to cancel my appointment" scenario. You're looking for the candidate to try to reschedule the patient.

Interview 3:

For the third interview, the candidate meets with your staff for a few hours. I pay particular attention to whether the candidate is engaged and asks questions. Better yet, does he/she take the initiative to help out? For example, if he/she is seeking a medical assistant position and is in the treatment room, does he/she shake hands with the patient and introduce himself/herself? Does he/she seem interested in what's going on?

This third interview reveals if I can get along with him/her, and it allows him/her to decide if he/she would like to work with our team.

Final Hiring Steps

After we get past the three-part interview process and check the candidate's references, I contact Real Talent Hiring for the final step. The owner, Jay Henderson, has developed the Hiring MRI formula to hire your next superstar. It isn't a personality profile or behavior assessment; it's an objective human performance metric that's tailored to fit your business's unique needs. The results of this test will help you decide if the candidate is the right fit for your company. You can hire someone who's smart and a real go-getter, but he or she might not fit in with your team and culture. Unless the candidate has taken this assessment, there's no way to know if he/she will fit until after he/she is hired.

This assessment takes the fear out of making a bad hire. Hiring the wrong person is extremely costly. Imagine that a staff member is working at only 60 percent of their potential. The hidden cost of this person could be that you're losing 40 percent of your potential business. Your bad hire could be chasing patients away. The test is inexpensive and the value is immense, so go the extra mile and give that candidate a Hiring MRI.

Next, you need to discuss salary and benefits. I hire only hourly employees. I know what I can afford and what the position is worth. Even if I'm hiring for an administrative position, I pay them by the hour for the first year. This gives you time to make sure they're a good fit before making them a salaried employee.

Never overextend yourself financially. Perhaps you found an amazing person, and he requests a salary that's higher than you can afford. Don't convince yourself that it will be worth it because he will be amazing, you won't have to train him that much, and he'll bring in extra revenue. That rarely happens. If the candidate makes demands before he's hired, there's a risk that he'll be demanding afterward. You don't need a thorn in your side.

Onboarding

Congratulations on hiring your future superstar, a new member of your "A" team! Now she needs to be taught how to do her job. Some offices make a mistake when they hire someone with experience. They simply show the person her new desk and say, "Here you go," expecting her to know what you want her to do. Don't do that. It doesn't matter how experienced she is; she must be trained. And her training must be identical to how you would train an inexperienced employee who is just learning the job. Start from the beginning.

At the beginning of every football season, the great Green Bay Packers coach, Vince Lombardi, would hold up a football and say, "Gentlemen, this is a football." He always went back to the basics. That's what you should do, too. Don't make any assumptions. Show your new employee the copy machine and teach her how to use it. Something that's simple for one person is not so simple for another. So, show her where everything is and how to use it.

Here's the checklist we use to ensure that our new hires are taught everything they need to know.

NEW HIRE CHECKLIST

- ☐ How to open the office
- ☐ How to close the office
- ☐ How to use the phones
- ☐ How to use the intercoms
- ☐ How to set and turn off the alarm system
- ☐ Give them a key
- ☐ Tell them the lounge rules
- ☐ How to use the computer
- ☐ How to use the credit card machine
- ☐ How to use the copier and replace the toner
- ☐ What to do if supplies are running low
- ☐ Location of the supplies
- ☐ How to fill out a time sheet
- ☐ Review their benefits with them
- ☐ How to request time off
- ☐ Teach them the importance of five-minute meetings
- ☐ How to triple-confirm appointments (mention the appointment three times)
- ☐ What to do when orthotics come in
- ☐ How to fill out a patient history form
- ☐ When and how to ask for referrals
- ☐ How to back up the computer
- ☐ How to route mail
- ☐ When and how to follow the recall system
- ☐ How to give directions to the office
- ☐ How to take a message
- ☐ How to give out referral packets
- ☐ How to clock in and out
- ☐ What to do in an emergency
- ☐ When it's okay to interrupt the doctor
- ☐ How to produce statistic sheets and graphs
- ☐ How to embrace our mission statement and purpose

Next, give your new hire a copy of the employee manual. This manual should describe all the employee benefits and policies, including which holidays are paid holidays and the number of vacation days, sick days, and paid time off days (PTO). It must also describe the procedure for calling in sick and for bereavement days.

The reason you have this manual is to establish standard procedures so that everyone is treated the same. No more making up rules as you go along. When someone asks for PTO, they fill out a form and the office manager follows the protocol in the manual to either approve or deny the request. It's that simple. If you want to see a copy of an employee manual, you can find it on my website at www.drpeterwishnie.com/resources.

Your new employee must read the manual, then sign and date each page. That makes them responsible for following your procedures. I learned this practice from a judge. A long time ago, I fired an employee and she took me to court. She said that I owed her vacation days. I brought the employee manual with me to small claims court. The employee brought an old manual with her, which was not the one I gave her. I won my case, but the judge suggested that I have each employee sign and date the bottom of each page. Further, whenever I update the manual, I have each staff member sign and date that page. Every year we review the manual, and the staff signs and dates it again.

Training for the Position

Next comes individualized training. My office manager—I call her my PAL, which stands for Practice Administrator Leader—is also my trainer. I learned to delegate training to someone else a long time ago. In fact, whenever I don't like doing something, and I don't have to be the one to do it, I ask, "How can I get this done extremely well without me?" The answer is to train one person who understands and follows all the systems and protocols in the practice to do it.

Sarah, my PAL, started off working with me as a patient care coordinator, then she was a medical assistant, and next she became the financial assistant. She can do every job in the practice, so she trains new employees on everything they need to know, including the computer system, the employee manual, the front desk activities, and even some financial duties.

Our lead medical assistants train the new medical assistants. We have checklists for each position (remember when we documented all job processes?), and we make sure our new hire is proficient in each area. Depending on the position, their training can take anywhere from a couple of weeks to a couple of months.

The hardest job is working the front desk. There are so many things that happen at the same time. The phones are ringing, patients are checking in, and patients are checking out. The front desk person must ask for money, put in payments, and write notes for gym, school, and work. They might know how to do every individual task, but putting the whole thing together and communicating well with the other front desk person takes time. So, don't rush the training. Everyone learns at a different speed. As long as the person takes responsibility for their job and reviews the work by studying at night, then everything will turn out fine.

The key is to streamline the processes. If your person makes too many mistakes, you might have to simplify the playbook. For example, there could be one check-in person and one check-out person. In busy offices, you can have a call center. This could be a group of people whose main job is to answer the phones and handle every call. They would be trained to answer the patient's questions and make appointments. They can also make calls to ask patients to pick up shoes and orthotics, and they can call patients who recently missed their appointments so they can be rescheduled. In my office, these people work in a private area.

Another way to streamline processes at the front desk is to have your medical assistants make follow-up appointments in the treatment rooms. There's less chatter in the treatment room compared to the front desk, and the medical assistants understand why the patients need to come back. The main reason why patients don't keep their follow-up appointments is that they're doing better and they don't understand the purpose of their next visit. The doctor and the person who makes the appointment must reiterate the purpose of their next visit. Doing this one thing helps ensure that your patients come back, which, in the long run, means more revenue for your practice.

That's why training is so crucial. Your new employee not only needs to know how to do a specific job, he or she needs to understand why they need to do it. It all goes back to the purpose of your practice. Since our mission is to SERVE the patients, we must show we care by helping them get better.

When a new hire is fully trained, we give them a quiz that has at least one hundred questions. The results show if the staff member is now competent. It also shows me, the doctor-owner, if I can trust him/her to do the job like I want him/her to do it. He/she has to answer all the questions correctly. If he/she fails any one of them, go back to it and ask again.

An example question could be: "Please demonstrate how to make a new patient appointment." Or you could role play with her about the questions to ask when making an appointment. You can find the quiz on my website, www.drpeterwishnie.com/resources.

Don't let a new hire answer the phones until she's thoroughly trained on the protocol, can answer the most common questions, and can properly make an appointment. Patients get frustrated when they're put on hold by someone who should be able to handle the call. Don't let this happen.

Ongoing Training

You might think that since your new hire is trained, everyone in your office is trained. Think again. It may be true, but it's only for the moment. Have you ever scratched your head and wondered why someone did something out of the ordinary, or totally forgot what to do? It happens all the time. Staff do what they need to do in order to get the job done at that moment. They don't think about the long-term consequences of changing the system on the fly. That's why you retrain your staff every month. Once again, they'll go through the tests mentioned above to give them a refresher.

By the way, we all cut corners from time to time. We do a job a certain way, but for some reason, we stop doing it that way. Or we leave out steps because it's easier. It's not that we're lazy; we think we're making things easier. For example, say that you send every new patient a thank you letter, but all of a sudden, you stop doing it. Then you see a dip in new patients and wonder why, and it's because you stopped sending out the cards. This is why retraining and system reviews are vital to your business.

Retraining has a second purpose, and that is to give you a chance to re-visit your systems. As we retest our team members, the trainer and trainee might decide that a certain process is no longer effective. They can brain-storm to come up with a new way to do something, then suggest the new way in a meeting. Retraining also gives the employee one-on-one time away from their post, which allows them to openly discuss their feelings about the practice and their role.

Now that you've hired, trained, and retrained your "A" team, you can lead them to be top performers on a consistent basis.

CHAPTER 5:

Grow with Leadership

"No one stands taller in the climb to success than when he bends over to help up someone else." – John Maxwell

Here's the secret to getting the life you want: leadership. Developing yourself as a leader will set you free and allow you to get home at a normal hour, so you can have dinner with your family and play with your children. No matter how great your practice might be, it can only reach new heights through great leadership. Without it, your practice is limited.

In my thirty years of practice, I've found that there's always stuff to do—even after I've completed my to-do list. In the earlier chapters, we talked about having a vision for your practice. But what about a vision for your *life*? Why do you actually go to work? To see patients? I don't think so. You go to work for one reason, and that's to create the life you so deserve. You work to provide a life for you and your family and to build a legacy.

However, we're doctors, and we chose this field to be helpful to others. Sometimes we forget to help ourselves until one day, usually in our forties, we wake up exhausted and no longer excited to go to work. We look at our insurance reimbursements and think, *Why do I work so hard for this measly little check? Is it really worth it?* We get hit with audits and staff issues, and we just want to crawl under a rock and hope it all goes away.

This is called *burnout*, and it happens when you try to do everything yourself.

Leadership is the answer to this problem. When you become a great leader and develop a great team around you, you can prevent and even cure burnout. It requires courage—courage to sit down and take a hard look at yourself to see how you can improve, both as a leader and as a person.

Here are my 9.5 successful traits of a great leader:
1. Leaders are great coaches.
2. Leaders are great communicators.
3. Leaders have great vision.
4. Leaders are great planners.
5. Leaders lead by example.

6.   Leaders are great listeners.

7.   Leaders lead best when the going gets tough.

8.   Leaders focus on solutions, not problems.

9.   Leaders ask great questions.

9.5 Leaders work on themselves daily.

1. Leaders Are Great Coaches

Medical practices have managers, usually just one office manager. But I never liked the term *manager* because it means that there's a person who manages the office, and people don't like to be managed. They like to be led—and they really like to be heard. For years I never had an office manager. Instead, I had a key leader for each department, someone who took charge of their position and understood how and why we did things.

I once had a financial administrator who took care of all the billings and receivables. Having been successful at that, I thought she'd be a good office manager. A lot of podiatry practices have their billers manage their practice, so Robbie was promoted to handle both positions. That's when the trouble began. She walked around the office and continually reported to me about what was going wrong. She'd tell me what so and so didn't do and what mistakes they'd made. It got really tiresome after a while.

One day I asked her, "What went right today?" I knew my numbers, and we were doing well, so something had to be going right.

Some people can always find something that's wrong. Nothing in life is perfect, and you'll get whatever you're looking for—whether it's positive or negative. If you're looking for what's wrong, you'll find it. By asking Robbie about what went right, it meant that she had to start looking for the good things, rather than the bad. But she couldn't seem to make that shift. After a while, I'd had enough of her negative reports and fired her. I don't keep negative people.

Leaders aren't managers. Leaders find good people and coach them to take things one step further. They coach them to be great team players and eventually great leaders in their own right. A coach has a playbook, which—for you—is your practice manual. A coach tells his players the plan for the day, the week, the month, and even the year.

Leaders train their team players on a consistent basis. A great leader hires great team players, but they don't stop there. They coach the players to be great. They don't say, "Here's your desk. Now go to work." They motivate their team to perform at their highest levels.

> A great leader hires great team players, but they don't stop there. They coach the players to be great.

A leader doesn't micromanage. They believe in their team. After their team members learn their jobs, the leader leaves them alone. They know they'll make mistakes, but that's the only way people learn. Most mistakes can be fixed, and the leader can use that experience to teach and coach the player. They should then implement systems to prevent further mistakes.

The leader understands that the team comes before the individual, and all decisions are made based on what's best for the team.

Leaders don't avoid conflict. He or she will use conflict to address issues and coach the person to perform their job better. In contrast, a manager avoids conflict and acts like the three monkeys—see no evil, hear no evil, and speak no evil. Conflict is a *good* thing. It's an opportunity to build a stronger practice, and it can make every team member better. If someone is having a bad day or has a complaint, do you avoid it, do you handle it, or do you pass the buck to the office manager?

When there's a conflict, a good leader spends time with the team member to listen to their views and ask questions. However, the goal is for the leader to prevent conflicts. It's not always possible, but when there's an office conflict, a good leader will implement a system designed to prevent it from recurring. Great leaders and coaches are proactive; they get involved before action is needed. Managers react and get involved only after problems crop up.

Next, leaders focus on their great performers, while managers tend to focus on the poor ones. It's easy to forget about the team player who's doing a bang-up job. Be sure to walk around the office and compliment your staff for doing a great job—and be specific about it.

For example, say something like, "Mary, that was absolutely amazing how you handled Mr. Jones. He left the office feeling great, and that's due to your great customer service. Thank you." Mary will feel energized and, on top of that, you've complimented her in front of her peers. When you spend time with your team members who are doing well, you can lead them to reach their maximum potential.

A leader can see the potential in others, but they also know when to tell an employee that it's not working out. They're not afraid to let this person go. The team must always come before the individual.

Coaches always practice and scrimmage to make their teams better. Managers rarely practice. Never train your team only once. Re-train and quiz your staff several times a year. The learning can either be done collectively or individually. When you approach it as a team effort, it can be a fun and healthy team-building exercise. No one really loves training, so be sure that your trainer is energetic, smiles a lot, and has fun—then passes that fun to the team.

2. Leaders Are Great Communicators

If you want your organization to grow, your communications must be open. If not, people will assume the wrong things and make up stories based on false conclusions. Explain the present state of the organization to your staff and tell them where the business is going. Help your people understand how they fit into the organization's plans—not just how they fit in the hierarchy, but how they can help the organization reach its goals.

Motivational guru Tony Robbins says there are six human needs, and *certainty* is one of them. People love to work for a stable organization because it gives them security. But we also have an opposing human need, which is *uncertainty*. When it comes to a business, uncertainty represents goals that are attainable but require imagination to reach them—in other words, how can you involve the staff in the creative process to help the company grow? People want to be involved, to be included, and to feel significant, and that happens through open communications.

The best communicators are extraordinary listeners who ask extraordinary questions.

The best communicators are extraordinary listeners who ask extraordinary questions. Harness the urge to interrupt others while they are speaking. We tend to assume that we know what the person's going to say, so we're eager to speak. Respect the other person and wait until they're finished making their point, even if it might be wrong. Ask your staff for their opinions on certain situations and what they'd do if they were running the show.

Communicate openly with your patients, too, and make every effort to get in agreement with them. If they don't like your treatment plan or don't understand it, they may be negative or forceful. Don't push back and disagree with them, unless you want to end up in an argument. You could lose the patient. But if you say, "Mrs. Jones, I understand why you're saying that. If I was in your shoes, I would feel the same way," then you show that you heard them and respect their position.

Another way to get in agreement is to repeat back what you heard the patient say. When you repeat back their concerns and agree about what the problem is, they'll be open to listening to you.

It's hard to have open and respectful communications with someone if you don't like them, so find a reason to like the person you're talking to. That doesn't mean you have to socialize with them; it means you have to find common ground for communication. Don't judge people. You're there to help others and to serve both your staff and patients. And if you can't help them, continue to show concern and refer them to another doctor who can.

This technique also works with your staff. Most problems in life are due to poor communication. The best way to prevent mistakes is to listen with intent. Be 100 percent present during the conversation. Put down your cell phone and turn away from your computer. Look them in the eye. Repeat back what they said, so you agree on the situation. Being fully present shows respect for the other person and shows that you care enough to listen.

Sometimes communication is challenging. For example, why does it seem like the staff asks you questions at the most inappropriate times, like when you're prescribing a medication or you're in the middle of treating another patient? The way to handle this is to look the person in the eye, smile, and say, "I'll be right with you. I just need two seconds to finish sending this prescription out." Don't do what I've done at times, which is saying, "Can't you see I'm in the middle of something?" If that happens, you need to apologize and use it as a teaching tool. Teach your staff to ask if it's okay to interrupt you and to respect your answer. Leaders aren't perfect, but they know when they're wrong, and they admit it.

Communication style can be specific to a person, so be aware that the same word might mean a certain thing to you but something altogether different to someone else. Where we were raised and how we used words in the past—in addition to cultural differences—determine how we interpret speech. For example, take the word manipulate. Is it positive or negative? Some people may think it's a negative word because it means to manipulate someone or something for one's personal gain. However, according to the Oxford Dictionary, manipulate also means to handle or control a tool, mechanism, or situation in a skillful manner. Both interpretations are correct. Don't jump to conclusions. Find out the person's intent in regard to the words they use.

If you are sincerely trying to help your patients and your staff, and you don't get defensive and argue with them, your communication will flow. The most important part of communication is listening.

3. Leaders Are Visionaries

Leaders have great vision, and they lead their team to embrace the vision. But first, the team has to buy into the leader. Once they believe in the leader, they can buy into the vision. In his book, *The 21 Irrefutable Laws of Leadership: Follow Them and People Will Follow You*, John Maxwell says, "As a leader, your success is measured by your ability to actually take the people where they need to go. But you can do that only if the people first buy into you."

You need to know where you want to take your practice. Do you want to add additional offices with more doctors and staff, or are you happy with a smaller practice? Do you have plans for your staff to grow larger? Whatever it is, your team should be involved and informed. You can't reach your goals without them, so lead them to buy into your vision and let them help you get there. That means you need to put your staff first. They'll want to know how your vision affects them. Does it mean longer hours, more travel between offices, and more pay?

When I put an EMR system in my office, I sat down with the staff and explained how it would make their lives easier. I said that I knew there would be some pain at first and that change wasn't easy. In fact, most people hate change. But when I explained the reason behind the change—which was to be able to retrieve patient information quickly and to spend more quality time with the patients—and how the change would make the office more efficient and deliver better health care with improved communication, the team bought into it.

Your vision also includes how you want your office to look and feel. How do you want your patients to feel when they enter your office, and how do you want your staff to feel when coming to work? Write down your visions and share them with your staff. Ask for their opinions about how you can achieve them. Ask what you could do to foster the desired feelings in your patients and staff.

Always try to mitigate the fear of the unknown. If you make a change without fully explaining the reason behind it, it can strike fear in the hearts of your staff.

Always try to mitigate the fear of the unknown. If you make a change without fully explaining the reason behind it, it can strike fear in the hearts of your staff. They might imagine things that aren't as you represented them and unintentionally spread rumors. I'm sure you've had a patient who was afraid of a procedure and, after you finished it, they said, "That was it?" The patient was afraid of the unknown. The same goes with your staff. Explain any changes in full detail, and don't leave anything to the imagination. Just be sure that the change is an improvement and not just for the sake of change.

Helen Keller once said, "The only thing worse than being blind is having sight but no vision." Leaders know where they're going, and they persuade others to follow. Great leaders see what they want, pursue it, and then help others see it. Take the time to dream and create a vision of your organization and then share it with your staff.

4. Leaders Are Great Planners

A lot of people live life unintentionally. They go through the motions and wonder why things are the way they are. They want more time, more money, and less stress, but they don't plan for it. Maybe they don't plan because they want the flexibility to do what they want whenever they want. Or perhaps they function with to-do lists and a wish list. *I wish I had… or, If I had more money, I could do whatever-whatever is on my wish list.*

It doesn't work like that. I've been a planner since high school. In podiatry school, I'd look at my schoolwork and see what I needed to do that day and for the next few days. Then I'd reverse engineer everything. Did I have an exam coming up? I would think, *My test is next Thursday, so I have seven days to get ready.* I'd want to be fully prepared in six days, so I could review the material on day seven.

My roommate thought I was nuts. One time he saw the schedule I'd made for myself. It went something like this:

- 8:00–9:00 study Biochemistry

- 9:00–10:00 Physiology

- 10:00–11:00 Anatomy, and so on. I left my plan on the desk and when I came back to it, I saw that my roomie had added:

- 11:00–11:15 Bowel Movement (I'm being delicate—he didn't use those exact words!)

I thought it was hilarious. Maybe I was too obsessive with my schedule, but the point of making a schedule is to give you flexibility.

As you get older, you'll have a lot more on your plate. If you want to strike a balance between your personal and professional life, then you need to plan.

Begin with your yearly goals. You should have yearly goals for your business, your health, your family, and for fun, as well as spiritual and mental goals. Next, turn these yearly goals into quarterly goals, so the year doesn't get away from you. Every new year, you might say, "This is going to be a great year. This is the year I'll make over a million dollars in my practice and pay off all of my debts." Then just like that, it's September and you're nowhere close to achieving those goals. It's because you didn't write out your plan for the million-dollar practice. It's a difficult goal, but when you break it down into quarterly goals and then monthly and weekly goals, it will appear a lot simpler and more achievable.

Be sure to use a really good planner—one that has a section for your yearly, monthly, weekly, and daily goals, plus a section where you can write down the big tasks that you'll do every day to achieve these goals. There will be a lot of them.

Some people focus on the minor tasks, but in order to achieve your yearly goals, you'll need to focus on the two to three major items that align with those goals. That's the real key. John Wooden, the greatest coach in the history of sports (who coached the UCLA men's basketball team to seven NCAA championships in a row) said the key to success is to do the little things consistently, and the way to do that is to plan what you need to do every single day.

5. Leaders Lead by Example

Have you heard the phrase, "Do as I say, not as I do?" The person who says this is not a true leader. Leaders have integrity.

If you want your staff to follow you and ultimately become leaders themselves, you need to set an example. There's no job too small for you to do. For example, if you're short staffed and you're ready to see the next patient but your medical assistant is busy with another patient, instead of sitting and waiting for someone to bring in the next patient, go out to the waiting room and invite the patient in yourself. If you see paper lying on the floor, pick it up. Do what you expect others to do.

If you tell your staff that your major core value for the organization is being honest and ethical but you're not honest with them, you'll lose their respect. That's not leading by example. Your core values can never be compromised.

If you tell your staff that your major core value for the organization is being honest and ethical but you're not honest with them, you'll lose their respect.

Whatever you ask your staff to do, you need to follow as well. Do you want your staff to arrive on time? Then be at work on time yourself. Do you treat your patients the way you want your staff to treat them or do you display a negative attitude? If you do, guess what? Your staff will, too. Integrity builds trust. Your staff will only follow you if they trust you. Let them watch you and do as you say *and* as you do.

6. Leaders Are Great Listeners

The best doctors, salesman, attorneys, etc. are great listeners. Listening is not as easy as it seems. As doctors, we want to cut to the chase and find out what the patient's main problem is. We don't want to hear what happened fifteen years ago. So, we interrupt and try to get the patient back on track.

The information we receive is based on the quality of the questions we ask. Just like a computer: garbage in, garbage out. However, when you interrupt, it seems rude to the patient—and it is. Studies have shown that about 75 percent of what you hear is heard incorrectly. When you interrupt or when you're not fully present, you miss clues that the patient is giving you. You may miss the true reason for their visit, and you definitely miss registering their tone and facial expressions. It's not only what your patients say, but also *how* they say it that gives you clues to how you can handle their problem.

When you interrupt your patients, it doesn't save time, it costs you time. You don't get the full meaning of what they're saying, and this is when mistakes can happen. Or more commonly, you don't address their issue. So, what happens? They call you back, and now you have to interrupt your day to return their call and spend extra time on the phone to actually listen to them. If you don't listen with intent the first time, you'll probably lose patients. Here are some tips to guide you to listen better:

- Stop talking. This is pretty obvious, but you might want to remind yourself to slow down and listen.

- Observe the patient's body language. Does it show that they're nervous, angry, or upset? Note their posture, facial expressions, gestures, movements, and eye contact. Ask the patient if something's bothering them. Let them know you're here to help, so they shouldn't be embarrassed to tell you the truth.

- If you must enter information into the computer and can't make direct eye contact, tell the patient what you're doing and that after you've entered the information, you'll give them your undivided attention.

- If the patient is sitting down—which they usually are—you should sit down, too, so you can maintain eye contact.

- Show empathy. Tell the patient you understand their situation. Be warm.

- Repeat what they told you. This is the how you understand the patient's main issue and show that you were listening.

- Be patient. Don't assume you know what the patient is going to say.

- Ask better questions. Ask questions that will give you the answers you're seeking.

Listening will make you a better doctor, will set the patient at ease, and will save you time. In addition, when you listen well, it increases the likelihood that the patient will refer a friend or family member to you.

But don't stop there! Take the time to listen to your people, too. You'll be a more empathetic, more understanding, and better leader.

7. Leaders Lead Best When the Going Gets Tough

It's easy to lead when things are going well, but a true leader shows up when problems arise. The key is not to focus on the problems but on the solutions to those problems. When problems occur, don't go negative. Pull yourself together and show your team that you've got this. Be confident that you can handle the problem. If you've been in practice long enough, you've probably had something negative happen, and you not only survived, but thrived.

I remember when my computer totally crashed. It happened over a President's Weekend. I had two hard drives that mirror imaged one another, so I thought that if one of them went down, I could access all the information on the other. That was not true. The second hard drive simply copied the information from the first one, so when the first drive went down, the second had nothing to copy. It was devastating.

After the initial shock wore off, I focused on solutions. We worked using paper and pen for a few days until my IT guy could replace the hard drives and put in a better backup system. Then, a few staff members and I worked over a weekend to input all the information we'd lost. We always had a paper trail, which helped a lot.

In times of trouble, stop and think. Don't panic. Leaders don't panic. They gather the troops and make things happen.

In times of trouble, stop and think. Don't panic.

Leaders have to make tough decisions. You might have to fire a well-liked employee. I once fired a very good worker due to sexual misconduct. He worked in our financial department and had helped bring in revenue.

He was very good at his job, but I didn't hesitate to fire him. I had to protect the rights of my employees and live up to our company ideals. It didn't matter that he was good at his job and people liked him.

Being a leader can be lonely. It's not your job to be liked. You're not looking for friends. You want your organization to thrive because, when that's the case, your team enjoys coming to work. No one wants to work for a failing company. People like to know that they're part of something that's working and that they're contributing to the organization's success. Thriving companies are usually happier companies. These companies are usually no-nonsense, and the work is meaningful both to the employees and the clients they serve.

Beware of staff who constantly ask you for favors or want something out of the ordinary. Can the company afford the new fandangled machine this person wants, and will this tool contribute to the company's bottom line or hinder it? You must decide what's right for your organization. Will granting this request help the company or hurt it? If you set this precedent, will others ask for similar favors?

You also have to take risks, because without taking risks, the company will never reach its full potential. This is why you must continually improve yourself. The team can only go as far you can take them. If you're limited in your vision and abilities, your team will be, too.

Before you have tough times, improve your decision-making skills and build up your confidence and experience. The best way to do this is to read from great leaders like John Maxwell, Michael Hyatt, Brendon Burchard, Jocko Willink, and John Wooden, to name a few. Further, hang around experienced and positive people who can teach and mentor you.

Building a thriving practice is not only about getting more patients. It starts with you and your leadership abilities.

8. Leaders Focus on Solutions, Not Problems

We all face problems and obstacles, but how you handle these situations determines whether you're a great leader or not. I used to fear these dreadful words: "Doc, we have a problem." My stomach would sink and become one big knot. Then guess what? The problem was never really that big. So now I have a golden rule: never say we have a problem. Come to me only when you have a solution.

When your staff crafts their own solutions, they feel empowered, especially when you take their solutions and run with them. In addition, it saves you time. Many times, these so-called problems arise when you're seeing patients and don't want to be disturbed. Being interrupted pulls you out of your rhythm and is disrespectful to the patient. You can eliminate that by insisting that the staff seek out their own solutions.

A good leader allows their team the freedom to find and implement solutions. When the going gets tough, you'll need to be fully present and take over the situation, but this doesn't mean that you leave your team out of it unless your problem is personal. Your team needs to be in the trenches with you, and they need to know you've got their back.

Within every obstacle lies an opportunity. When a problem crops up, think to yourself, *What's good about this?* Perhaps a patient is suing you for malpractice, even though you know you did everything right. Ask yourself, *What's good about this?* When you sit down to review your interactions with this patient, you may discover that you'd been rushing around and didn't give this patient the proper time and attention he/she needed. Determine that from now on, you'll make a point to maintain better eye contact with your patients and develop a better rapport. You'll follow up with them to make sure they keep their appointments. You realize that patients are more likely to sue you if they don't like you—and perhaps this lawsuit had nothing to do with your surgical skills. Then you can move through your day with a positive attitude and a smile on your face because you've figured out the solution to deter further lawsuits.

That's what a good leader does. You brush off adversity and look for the good in everything. Otherwise you can wind up miserable and depressed.

9. Leaders Ask Great Questions

Leaders never make assumptions. Leaders ask their team about what's happening, why it's happening, and how can you can—as a team—prevent it from happening again. Leaders don't tell people what to do; they direct them toward success. They don't order people around. When your staff comes to you with a problem, ask them, "What would you do? How would you handle this?" Then let them to run with it.

However, their solutions won't always be right. Let's say you asked your front desk person why a patient cancelled his appointment, and he/she didn't try to reschedule. The policy is to find out why a patient wanted to cancel and to reschedule them. Patients frequently cancel because they misunderstand the treatment process or have heard through the grapevine that orthotics—or another treatment you've suggested—doesn't work. These misunderstandings happen more often than you think. When you don't attempt to reschedule the appointment, the patient can feel like the office doesn't care about him or her.

But your front desk person didn't follow the protocol, and how you deal with the situation is important. Do you go nuts and get upset? Or do you ask questions and stay calm?

Start by asking why he/she didn't try to reschedule the patient. Try not to make him/her feel bad. You don't want him/her to be defensive. Ask him/her, based on the office procedures, what the best approach is to handle a patient who wants to cancel their appointment. Review the practice's mission statement and the vision of the organization. Don't do this in front of the other staff members, and certainly not during patient hours. Maintain the attitude that every mistake is not a mistake; it's a teaching opportunity.

If you're truly interested in your team, you'll show that you genuinely care about them. People will follow your leadership when—and only when—they know how much you care about them. Ask for their help when you need it, ask for their opinions, ask how you can improve a situation. Get all the information you need to make better decisions.

Tony Robbins says that if you want a better answer, ask yourself a better question. For example, how can I get all of my medical notes entered on time without added stress and without falling behind my schedule? Your subconscious mind will immediately start working to find the right answer. You just need to be specific about what you want.

9.5 Leaders Improve Themselves Daily

I made this a half-step because, if you're following the other nine steps, you're already working on yourself. However, there's more to do.

The world is full of negativity, but you don't have to buy into that. The doctors around you are negative, the patients are negative, maybe some of your staff—and definitely the news—is negative. Don't watch the news unless you want to start your day being negative and full of anger. Do you know what CNN stands for? Constant Negative News. So, instead of turning on the television first thing in the morning or immersing yourself in social media, do what most successful millionaires do. Successful people have an established morning routine that helps them focus on the important things that make a big difference.

This is how I spend my morning: I get up at 4:30 a.m. and drink two glasses of water. We all get dehydrated overnight and need to rehydrate. I then drink coffee with MCT oil. This wakes up my brain. Next, I write down three to five things that I'm grateful for in my gratitude journal. Like everyone else, I could focus on what I don't have, but thinking about what I'm grateful for makes me feel better. People who are depressed regularly focus on what they don't have, so when you feel down, stop and think about all the great things you have. Write down simple things like, *I'm grateful that it's spring and the flowers are blooming, the sun is out, my children are healthy, and I have gas in my car that takes me to work.* Don't take anything for granted.

After that, I meditate for about five minutes. I must admit that this isn't easy, so I have several ways I go about it. Sometimes I just relax, light a candle, close my eyes, and try not think about a thing. When my thoughts come in, I just let them, but then I regroup. I want to free up my mind and get myself in a relaxed state. Studies have shown that if you have a problem you're trying to solve, you should meditate. When you relax your mind, it allows your brain to accept new ideas that can help you. It's very hard to come up with ideas and solutions when you're not in a relaxed state.

When you relax your mind, it allows your brain to accept new ideas that can help you.

On other days, I listen to meditation music and read my goals and affirmations. Either way, I review my goals every morning. The more often you look at your goals and recite them with enthusiasm, the more likely they are to happen. Some of my affirmations are: *Things come easy to me, I listen intently to my patients, and money flows easily to me.*

Next, I review my plan for the day, and I write down the top three things I must do that align with my goals. If I do those three things and nothing else, then it will be a good day. For example, while I was writing this book, I wrote in my planner, *Write five hundred words today.* That was one thing I needed to do to finish writing the book. Then I'd read anywhere from five to ten pages in a good self-help or business book. After that, I'd head to the gym around 6:30 a.m. and be ready for my day to start at 9:00 a.m.

You might think this is a lot to do, and some of you can't do all of this in the morning. That's okay. Just do what you can. Establish a morning routine that includes planning your day, showing gratitude, and reviewing your goals. The point is to make it a habit. When I don't follow this routine, I feel lost, and I'm more likely to be overwhelmed.

I believe in the CANI principle that Tony Robbins teaches: Constant And Never-ending Improvement. We'll never be perfect, but we can always be better. Being a better leader means that you take care of yourself first, then you teach others. When you teach others to lead, it will set you free and give you the time you want to spend with your friends and family. Remember why you own a practice: to give you the life that you so deserve.

CHAPTER 6:
Setting Goals

"To accomplish our goals, we must distill our dreams into daily actions."
– Michael Hyatt

Maybe you've heard about the value of setting goals. Most everyone has. The problem is that most people don't have goals, and if they do, they don't write them down.

Goals are different from resolutions. It's common to make resolutions every new year. *I'm going to quit smoking, lose weight, get out of debt*, and so on. The difference between setting goals and making resolutions is that goals are written down, and resolutions are simply dreams or wishes. A goal that's not written down is just a dream.

There've been a lot of books written about goal setting, and I've read a lot of them. You may have, too, or you might be new to the practice, or you might not want to set goals. This chapter will teach you about the true power of setting goals.

First, think about your day. You get up and go to work. But why do you do that; why do you go to work? Of course, it's to put food on the table, clothes on your children, and a roof over your heads. But here's the thing: I'm sure you didn't suffer through all those years of podiatry school and residency to simply survive.

You probably had aspirations to live a really good life. You thought about the kind of house you wanted, the car you'd like to drive, and the vacations you would take. So, do you go to work to provide yourself with the basics, or do you go to work to help people get out of their pain? My guess is that you became a doctor to help people, but you also want to be well-rewarded for your efforts. Your immediate goal is to pay all the bills and take home whatever is left. And you hope that's a lot!

There's a universal law that says you'll make only what you need and nothing more. That means that if you want to make a lot more than you need, you'll need to trick the universe into thinking you truly need this money.

How do you do that? Let's say you've budgeted $50,000 per month to pay all your office bills, including your salary. In order to make $75,000 a month, you have to put that figure in your budget. You have to tell the universe that you need $75,000. You can designate the additional $25,000 as a bill that you pay to yourself. But don't include the full $75,000 in the budget at first. Budget for 10 percent over your actual figure, which is $5,000. Increase this figure every month by $5,000 until you've budgeted for the full $75,000.

What you just did was set a goal—a goal that you must make $75,000 a month. You put the goal into action when you wrote it down and figured out how to make an additional $5,000 that month. How many more new patients do you need to see, how many orthotics do you need to make, and what should your production look like to meet the goal?

Maybe you've tried setting goals before and weren't successful. There's always a reason for this. First, you probably didn't believe in the goals. They sounded great, but you didn't know anyone who had achieved what you want. Or if they did, maybe you thought it was because their spouse was wealthy, or their family was rich, or they had great investments. You may have a belief that podiatrists need to work their butts off to make a good living and that they can't become rich.

Or you might believe that you don't deserve all the good things you want. Perhaps you have a false belief that you can't be a good businessperson because you don't have the experience or knowledge. Maybe you believe that money is bad and that people with lots of money are greedy—and you don't want to be like that.

When someone is greedy, it's simply a sign that they have a scarcity mentality. The truth is that there's enough money for everyone, but many people have an underlying belief that if they become rich, it means that someone else has to be poor. The truth is that money, in the hands of good people, will help them do good things. The opposite is also true. When money's in the hands of bad people, it will support them in being bad. Zig Ziglar said that the more people you help, the more money you'll have. I believe that, too.

If you're afraid to fail, setting goals won't work. *What will people think if I tell them my goals and dreams and I fail? Will they laugh at me and say, "I told you so"?* The only way to reach your goals and have your dreams come true is to take risks.

The only way to reach your goals and have your dreams come true is to take risks.

The most successful people in the world have taken risks and failed. Thomas Edison failed at inventing the light bulb over one thousand times, but he didn't give up. People thought he was crazy and that he should forget his ridiculous invention. Abraham Lincoln was defeated for state legislature; he failed in business; his sweetheart died; he had a nervous breakdown; he was defeated for speaker of the Illinois House of Representatives, then defeated for a nomination for U. S. Congress; he was defeated for U.S. Senate; and defeated for the nomination for vice president of the United States—but eventually he became president.

Another reason setting goals may not have worked for you is because your *why* isn't big enough. Going to work for the sole purpose of making money isn't enough. You need a purpose. That purpose can be to help people, but podiatrists don't simply help people with their foot and ankle problems; we actually give people back their quality of life. Their feet are critical for staying mobile and active, which helps them stay young and healthy. That alone could keep you motivated.

You're going to have good days and bad days. There will be days when you say, "I'm done," and, "This is impossible." But if your *why* is super strong and invokes an emotional response in your head and gut, you'll stay the course. Without this deep, internal feeling, you'll most likely quit.

In order to find your *why*, ask yourself some important questions and drill down to the base answer. Ask yourself the question, "Why?" seven times. Here's an example.

"Why do you want to be successful in life?"

You might answer, "Security."

Then ask, "Why is it important to have security?"

Your answer: "No stress."

Ask again. "Why is it important not have stress in my life?"

Your answer: "So I won't have to worry about money and I'll have freedom."

Ask again. "Why is it important to have freedom and not worry about money?"

Your answer: "To be able to control my life and do what's important and to do what I want instead of what other people want me to do."

Then the fifth why: "Why is it important to have control?"

Your answer: "So I can help more people and be there for the people I love."

Again, you ask, "Why is it important to help more people?"

Your answer: "Because it feels good and it makes me feel worthwhile."

Then comes the final why: "Why is it important to feel worthwhile?'

Your answer: "I never want to think small. I want to know that no matter what obstacles come, I can not only handle it, but I can overcome it and become a great success. I also want to teach my children not to give up and to make their dreams big and bigger, so they always have choices."

As long as you emotionally connect with your *why*, you'll achieve your goals and dreams. People lose their way when they lose their *why*. Steve Jobs said, "If you're not passionate enough from the start, you'll never stick it out."

Further, your *why* is to provide a high quality of life for you and your family. What that means will differ from person to person, so the key is to figure out what you want and to visualize having it. One of the best ways to do this is to create a vision board that has pictures of what you want your life to look like. Include pictures of your family on vacation, a representative photo of the kind of house you'd like to live in, pictures of activities you like to do, the charities that interest you, and a picture of your practice with smiling, happy people working in it.

Many people became successful by visualizing what they wanted. Before he was a household name, Steve Harvey read a note to himself every day that he wrote when he was a child. It said, "I'm going to be on TV." When he was twenty-three, Jim Carey, the great actor and comedian, wrote himself a check for $10 million for acting services rendered. He postdated it for ten years later and kept it in his wallet. And when he was thirty-three, he earned $10 million for the movie *Dumb and Dumber*. The top-ranked golfer, Jack Nicklaus, attributed his success to visualizing every single shot he made. He pictured his back swing, how the head of the golf club struck the ball, the flight of the ball, the ball's landing, and how the ball rolled to the exact spot where he wanted it to go.

After my divorce and a breakup with a girlfriend, I decided to sit down to think about what type of woman I wanted in my life, and I listed the qualities she would have. I wouldn't settle for her having nine out of ten; I wanted someone who had all ten qualities for us to be happy together. I put the list on my vision board and saw it every morning. I tasked my subconscious mind with finding this woman, and I'm thankful that I've now found her.

Visualization has been proven to stimulate the muscles to perform physical actions, and it also programs the mind to increase your confidence and relax your body. It improves your concentration because you focus on the events that will help you achieve your goals.

Believe in the power of making goals! Life doesn't just happen; you must live with intention. You can be the architect of your own life and design it the way you want it to be, just like Michelangelo designed his art.

I use an exact system to set goals. Many people have followed it, and if you do, too, I guarantee that you will reach your goals. It's called the S.M.A.R.T. system, but I actually like how Michael Hyatt has extended that to become the S.M.A.R.T.E.R. system. Here's how it works:

1. **S stands for *specific*.** What exactly do you want? Broad, vague goals are only a starting place. They don't give you the direction and daily intentionality you need to achieve them. You need to get specific. For example, by December 31st—or sooner—my organization will have collected $1 million or more.

2. **M stands for *measurable*.** Measurable goals are much easier to achieve than ones that cannot be measured. They allow you to gauge your progress and make adjustments along the way. Otherwise, you have no idea how you're actually doing—until you fail to achieve your goal. Continuing with the above example, measure how much money you're making daily, weekly, and monthly, and then consult those numbers to determine if you're on track or if you need to make changes.

3. **A stands for *achievable*.** Goals that aren't achievable will only frustrate you and will make it far more likely that you'll give up too soon. You need something that's a stretch but is possible to achieve. For example, if you want $1 million in revenue by the end of the calendar year, and you now collect $500,000 per year, can you really double your income in a single year?

   And beware of aiming too low with your goals. If you underestimate yourself so you can achieve a goal, you won't rise to your full potential. Make your goals achievable while still stretching you out of your comfort zone. If your goals are too easy, you'll get bored.

4. **R stands for *realistic*.** This goes hand in hand with setting achievable goals. You might have plenty of otherwise achievable goals that aren't realistic for you at this point in time. When you try to conquer too many goals at once, they all become hard to achieve. Other factors can also render your goals unrealistic. For example, say you're pretty sure you could double your income in a calendar year, but your partner suddenly retired for health reasons and you can't replace him for a while. At this particular time, the goal to increase your income by 100 percent may be temporarily unrealistic.

   R is also for *risky*. Successful people take risks, but these risks are well thought out and calculated. Dream big and take some chances, but make sure you don't commit to something you can't get out of.

In 1519, Captain Hernan Cortes landed in Veracruz to begin his great conquest. Upon arriving, he gave the order to his men to burn the ships. There was no turning back, no safety net; they had to achieve the conquest. Either they would succeed or they would die.

That's a huge risk, and I'm not saying you should go those extremes. For example, say you want to grow your practice by 20 percent this year, but you know you'll need more staff to do so. In this case, you shouldn't wait to hire the staff. It takes time to find the right team players and to train them. Hire them immediately, and you'll see the growth. Build it and they will come; don't wait for them to come to build it.

5. **T stands for *time-bound*.** Your goals must have a specific end date, so you keep yourself focused and don't procrastinate. If you don't have an end date, you may never reach your goal. Or it could take much longer than it should.

6. **E stands for *exciting*.** Exciting goals inspire you. Studies have shown that enjoyment is the key factor to success. Your goals must personally inspire you, so you'll stay motivated when times get tough.

7. **R stands for *relevant*.** Your goals should be relevant to your life. If you aim to do too much at one time, you'll get overwhelmed. So, evaluate the current demands on your time and understand your values. If you have family or other obligations and your goals don't align with your values, you'll magnify your stress. Make sure that all your goals align with one another.

Write down separate goals for each area of your life, such as your business, your finances, your health, your family, and even fun goals. Set goals for these areas for this year and for three years and five years out. This exercise is sometimes difficult, so I've included a link at the end of this chapter to download goal worksheets from my website.

If you don't set goals, the years will fly by without a plan. First, it's January, and the next thing you know, you're eating Thanksgiving dinner. If you don't plan for change, you won't attain your life goals. It's not the actual planning of goals that causes anxiety and frustration; frustration comes when you haven't acted on them.

To get started, take your annual goals and divide them into what you need to achieve in each quarter (thirteen weeks) to achieve them. Next, take your quarterly goals and break them down into weekly goals and then into daily goals.

Every Sunday night I plan for the week ahead. As Steven Covey teaches in his classic book, *The Seven Habits of Highly Effective People*, it's best to plan for the big rocks first. The big rocks are things that take care of you and give you more energy—energy that keeps you at the top of your game when you're dealing with your staff and patients, family and friends. These rocks include proper nutrition, exercise, vacation time, meditation, and reserving time to plan. These are your "me times." They come first.

To have this "me time," you have to control your calendar. For example, I write down my workouts in my planner. I reserve time for my morning and evening rituals there, too. Then I block off my patient hours. My surgery schedule is different each week, so I block off time for that.

Next, focus on the roles you play in life. You're a parent, a son or daughter, a friend, a boss or employee, a doctor, and a spiritual being. You won't necessarily do something to fulfill all these roles every week, but these relationships are important, so prioritize them. I write down my scheduled plans, like going to the game with my sons or having dinner with my girlfriend, as priorities in my planner. These are the big rocks—rocks that maintain healthy relationships and increase the bonds with the people you love.

Now you can work on your business. What will you do to market your practice this week? What financial reports and analyses will you evaluate? What will you discuss at your weekly staff meeting. Will you meet with your bookkeeper, billing person, or marketer? Do you have agendas for these meetings? What goals will you set for your team this week to align with your quarterly and yearly goals? How will you lead your people to achieve these goals? This seems like a lot, but when you get started and make this weekly planning a habit, it will only take you thirty minutes to an hour to do it.

Remember that your goals are SMARTER ones, and the M stands for measurable. You must keep score and be accountable for your actions. If you planned to go to the gym four times this week, how successful were you? If you decided that something else was more important and you were only able to go three times, don't knock yourself down. If you skipped exercise to do something with your children, then be proud that you're making good decisions based on what matters most. But if you skipped the gym to watch reality TV and eat bonbons, don't make a habit of it. Don't say, "I can do it tomorrow." Do it now! You'll feel a lot better when you accomplish the things that are important to you.

You're going to have a lot of wins along the way, so be sure to celebrate them! If your goal for the month is to collect $100,000 and the month is half over and you've already collected $50,000, have a mini-celebration with the staff. Bring in lunch and celebrate that you're halfway there. Thank them, but remind them that this isn't the time to take the foot off the pedal. Promise them a surprise when the final goal is achieved, which could be something as simple as a $25 gift card.

It's hard to reach your goals without accountability. Tell your friend, your spouse, or a mentor what your goal is and check in with them weekly. I'm not only accountable to myself, but to my coach. Coaches need coaches. I coach many people, and I give them homework assignments. These assignments get them closer to their goals. We check in regularly to assess their progress. You're more likely to achieve your goals if you're accountable because nobody wants to disappoint or be embarrassed in front of other people.

Constantly improve and do better every single day. There's no arrival, no destination—so enjoy the journey! You can always continue to grow and succeed, even if what you pursue changes. According to author and speaker Earl Nightingale, success is a progressive realization of a worthy ideal. There's no official end.

Success is the farmer who's growing crops because that's what he wants to do. Success is the entrepreneur who starts her own company because that was her dream. Success is a physician who is living the kind of life he or she wants to live, no matter what their bottom line is. Enjoy your journey.

Keep your purpose in mind and you'll always have goals to set and strive toward.

I invite you to visit www.drpeterwishnie.com/resources to print out the goal worksheets and to start writing your goals right away.

CHAPTER 7:

Communicate for Success

"The single biggest problem in communication is the illusion that it has taken place." – George Bernard Shaw

Most of the problems in your office are either caused by miscommunication or a lack of communication. It takes time and effort to remedy communication problems, and this chapter will give you some tried-and-true tips to make your office communications flow easier.

It starts with great listening.

When you listen first, it helps to understand the other person. You need to know what your staff and patients want and need from you, and the only way to learn that is to listen to them. Not half-hearted, unfocused listening, but *active* listening. Maintain excellent eye contact at all times, then repeat back what he or she said to you to confirm that you heard what was said. Never interrupt a patient or staff member who's speaking.

Here's an example. Let's say a patient is really upset because he had to wait a long time to see the doctor. He's so upset that he yells at the receptionist. Your receptionist should already have been trained to maintain her cool and stay attentive. When the patient finishes yelling—and eventually he'll stop—the receptionist must reply to him with the same verbiage he used, in a similar firm tone, but without yelling. She could say, "What I'm hearing is that you're quite upset because you've been waiting for forty-five minutes and you have another appointment elsewhere. Is that correct, Mr. Jones?" The patient will agree, and now your receptionist must *agree with him* by saying, "Mr. Jones, this isn't acceptable, and I'd be upset, too, if I had to wait this long."

Next, she needs to resolve the situation. She can find out how much longer it will be, make the doctor aware of the situation, and ask if they can see the patient immediately. If so, bring the patient in ASAP, but don't charge him for the visit. You can charge the insurance for the services, but don't charge the evaluation and management code. Offer the patient snacks and beverages. A gift card to Dunkin' Donuts or Starbucks would be good, too. If you can't see the patient right then, reappoint him with a free exam and offer him a gift card. That night, you should call the patient to apologize.

The key points are to listen with intent, make good eye content, match the tone level of the patient, never be condescending, repeat back what the patient said to you, make sure the patient agrees that you understand the issue, and handle the situation immediately.

It's not enough to be a great doctor. Successful people are great communicators. Great leaders are great communicators because they easily relate to people. To have the practice of your dreams that provides you with the lifestyle you so deserve, you need to lead people and communicate with them—not only with your patients, but with your staff, other physicians, and anyone else you might meet.

First, you must care about the person. Learn about them and show them you're deeply interested in them. Ask questions and listen intently. If you only care about getting your point across, that's not communication. That's a monologue. If that happens, they won't do business with you, or they won't be able to relate to you, or they simply won't want to be around you.

Remember: you don't treat feet and ankles, you treat people. People buy from you because of how much you care, not because of how much you know. You may have completed a three-year or even a four-year top-notch residency program. You can repair an ankle fracture with your eyes closed, but it doesn't matter unless the patient has complete trust in your abilities. You have to connect with the patient on an emotional level, which only happens with good communication. Connection is what develops relationships. Zig Ziglar, the famous motivational speaker and author, said, "If you help enough people get what they want, you'll get what you want."

Think about how you enter the treatment room. Do you say, "What seems to be bothering you?" Or, do you develop a rapport with the patient instead? If you want them to get better quickly, get to know them first. Your patient isn't just someone with a foot and ankle problem. Everything in the body is connected. Find out what's bothering them and learn how their foot problem prevents them from doing what they want to do. How does this issue impact their day?

To develop rapport, introduce yourself, shake their hand, and say your name slowly when you enter the treatment room. I'm astounded at how many times I've heard patients say that they don't remember their previous doctor's name. That's definitely a marketing problem, but it's also sort of ridiculous if they don't know your name by the time they leave your office. I usually like to say something stupid so they can remember my name like, "Hello, my name is Dr. Peter Wishnie, like make a wish on your knee." It's stupid, but they won't forget it—and now you also know how to pronounce my name! This is especially important if you have an unusual sounding name.

Next, I sit down so I can make eye contact with the patient. I ask questions to get to know her better, rather than immediately looking at my computer. I ask if she had any trouble finding the office, what kind of work she does—and depending on the situation—I learn more about her life, such as her family and hobbies. Then I turn to her foot problem. I ask her how her foot problem affects her life, and I ask about her goals and expectations for her treatment. Of course, the ultimate goal is for her to get better, but she could have a wedding or a vacation she has planned, and she wants to be 100 percent by that time. It's important to understand her expectations because you may need to steer those expectations in a more realistic direction while, at the same time, showing empathy. Continue to ask questions throughout the exam and to make excellent eye contact.

But there's a lot more to communication than asking questions. Words represent only 7 percent of our communication. The way we say these words—our tone—represents 38 percent of our communication, and how we say them—our body language—is a whopping 55 percent of our communication. Over 90 percent of communication is non-verbal. In order to get your message across to your patients, you need to maintain good eye contact, have good posture, and the proper voice inflections.

Before you leave the exam room, ask the patient if there are any further questions or concerns. Don't do this with your hand on the doorknob! Never be in a rush to leave the room. Of course, sometimes you'll need to redirect the conversation in order to stay on topic and expedite the visit, but always do that with love. If he/she goes on and on about some information that doesn't relate to his/her foot problem, say, "I'm so sorry to interrupt, and I'd definitely love to hear more about that, but I have a very important question to ask you." Use the question you ask next to redirect him/her back to his/her foot problem. Then say that you have some very important information to tell him/her. When you do that, he/she will start listening to you.

The communication with your patients doesn't end with the visit. Continually reach out to them, so they'll keep coming back and refer other patients. I recommend that you call all your new patients the next day and ask them if they have any additional questions. Use this time to remind them of the purpose of their next appointment. I also send all new patients a new patient letter, thanking them for trusting us to take care of them. This letter should also document their diagnosis and treatment plan. I learned this in my residency from one of my mentors, Dr. Irv Donick. He told me this kind of letter is great for marketing purposes, but it's also great for legal reasons. By documenting the treatment plan and reminding the patient to take certain medications or to follow certain instructions, the patient can never say you didn't inform them, especially if a complication occurs.

It's true that we live in a whirlwind of communication and everyone gets sidetracked, especially with all the distractions of social media. We're constantly on our phones or thinking about things we need to do, so it's a rare person who can stay focused for long periods at a time. That's why you'll need to constantly communicate with your patients if you want them to follow their treatment plan and refer other patients to your practice. Letters, phone calls, newsletters, e-mails, and even texts are great ways to communicate with your patients.

You might worry that if you bombard them with too much information, they'll get mad. But if the content speaks directly to them, this won't be a problem. Sure, you'll get a few who will unsubscribe, but the majority don't mind. In fact, some of your messages won't even reach the patient because they'll get lost in the hundreds of messages they receive daily.

The key is to make the message about that particular patient. Send communications about heel pain to the patients who suffer heel pain; send patients who have bunions information about bunions. You can easily set up these types of campaigns with most CRM software. The marketing team in our office handles this, and when we see a new patient, they enter the diagnosis in that patient's record and enroll them in the appropriate campaign.

Proper communication involves:

1. First, listen with intent. This can also be done with a neuro-linguistic programming (NLP) technique called mirroring.

   Mirroring means that you mimic the other person's behaviors. In other words, if their arms are folded, you fold yours; if their hands are on their hips, so are yours. Of course, you wouldn't want to mirror them at exactly the same time because it will seem obnoxious. If done properly, the other person won't realize what you're doing. Studies have shown that this technique is extremely effective for good communication.

   Mirroring isn't strictly physical. You can also mirror the other person's tone, which we've already touched on. If they're upset and are raising their voice, raise your tone and put more energy into your voice. If the person is sad, lower your tone, but if they're bubbly, then be bubbly too.

2. Get to know the person you're talking to. Use the acronym FORM: Family, Occupation, Recreation, and Motivation. Start conversations by asking about these areas of his or her life. This kind of small talk gives

you an opportunity to get to know others and allows them to open up and share important information with you.

3. Don't use medical jargon. Stay away from the big fancy words. Just write down the actual diagnosis and other medical terms, and give it to the patient so they can Google it at home or have the information in case they want to research it. But when you explain their medical problem, use lay terms and try to make analogies. I'd say, "You have inflammation, or swelling, in your tendon that we call tendonitis." I tell them why they have it and use my foot model or diagrams to explain the condition. I also have pre-made treatment folders for my top thirty diagnoses. Each folder contains information on the problem with pictures, a page or two on the possible treatment plans, and information about our practice. When I give them the folder, I say, "Your husband/wife will ask you what the doctor said. Just hand him/her this folder."

4. Be polite and respectful. Too many doctors don't say please or thank you to their staff, and they particularly leave out these courtesies in the operating room. They yell, "Scalpel!" but it's a lot nicer and more respectful to say, "Scalpel, please," and then thank them. Use your manners. You're a leader and people follow your lead—and trust me, people are watching. If you train residents, they're watching and listening. So are your children and your staff. Lead by example. Remember to use the magic words!

5. Perfect your non-verbal communication. Always maintain great eye contact and good posture, without fidgeting or swaying. This is important no matter what the situation, but it's especially important when trying to sell a patient on your services. When discussing the cost of your services with the patient, you may get nervous and either slip in some "ums" or start fidgeting. This demonstrates a lack of confidence, and no one buys anything from people who aren't confident or aren't certain that the value of their services exceeds the price. Would you want a doctor who isn't sure of himself to operate on you?

When you talk to people, be it staff or patients, put yourself in their shoes. How would you like to be treated? How would you feel if you were in their situation? Don't assume you know how they feel and what they want—always ask questions to find out.

Proper communication is the key to your success.

Do you have a tough patient? You know the one—he or she constantly gives you a hard time or complains, even if you go above and beyond for them. They can ruin a good day, and your mood immediately changes when you see his or her name on your schedule. The truth is that nobody can ruin your day unless you let them. Simply focus on all your other patients who appreciate you. Always take the high road as you learn how to deal with this kind of person. As long as you are courteous and nice and you do your best to help this patient, you can go to sleep at night and feel good.

CHAPTER 8:

It's All in the Numbers

"Perfect numbers like perfect men are very rare." – Rene Descartes

Not everyone is a numbers person. I actually love this topic, and I love numbers, and here's why: If I told you that your practice can run effectively and efficiently and that you can know what's going on—even when you aren't physically present—would you want to learn how?

That's why knowing your numbers is important. Most doctors or office managers walk around and micromanage their staff. You look over the shoulders of your team members and try to be helpful, but that actually makes the staff feel like you don't trust them. When you know your numbers, you and your staff will know where to focus.

Remember, you're a coach, and a good coach has a game plan that he or she gives the team. That game plan should be based on strategy and your key performance indicators (KPIs), meaning your analytics. Why do your numbers go up one week and down the next? Most doctors don't even look at their numbers until the end of the month, and then they wonder why they can't pay the bills. Knowing your numbers will also keep you on track in regard to your goals. If you set goals and don't look at your numbers every day, you won't know if you should change direction or stay on course.

Let's say you need to see five new patients in order to meet your daily production goals. In my office, my marketing director goes over our major goals each morning. If she sees that we only have three new patients scheduled, she uses our intra-office email to tell everyone to schedule at least two more new patients. Then when the next new patient calls the office, our staff tries to get that person in that day.

The whole team is focused on our daily goals, but there's always one key number that's the lead measure. This is the number that, if achieved, will affect everything else. All you have to do is totally focus on this one number to reach most of your goals. In podiatry, the key number is to see new patients. They come in for a specific problem, we get them better, then they move on until they have another issue. So, we need a constant influx of new patients in order to have a thriving practice. New patients lead to an increase in production, which leads to an increase in collections and an increase in per visit value.

In podiatry, the key number is to see new patients.

What numbers do you need to know and, better yet, how do you interpret them?

The four key metrics I look at include the following:
- Production
- Collections
- New Patients
- Total Visits

- **Production:** This is your charges. I know that every office is different, and what one doctor charges is different from another. Plus, in a managed care society, it doesn't matter how much you charge because you can only collect what the insurance companies allow—unless you have a concierge practice and don't accept insurance. That being said, production is important because if you know how much you collect on the dollar, then you can figure out how much money you should receive in the near future. For example, if your collection ratio is 57 percent and you produced $100,000 in the month, then you can expect to receive $57,000. As an owner, you're not getting a straight salary, so it's good to know how much you need to produce to pay your bills.

- **Collections:** The importance of collections is pretty obvious because this is your bottom-line number. Everything you want to do professionally and personally hinges on this number.

- **New Patients:** As mentioned above, podiatry is totally dependent on seeing new patients. New patients are also your marketers, because if you *WOW!* them with great service (see chapter 10), they'll tell others to come to you. If you treat your patients with unbelievable service and get them better quickly, they'll tell everyone else about you. Because they're potential referrers and they generate the biggest per visit value, new patient numbers are your lead marker.

  This book doesn't fully address marketing to attract new patients. For that, I highly recommend *Podiatry Prosperity: How to Market, Manage, and Love Your Practice* by Rem Jackson and *It's No Secret . . . There's Money in Podiatry* by Tyson Franklin.

- **Total Visits:** This number isn't as important as the other three. You can see a lot of patients and, by the end of the day, you still might not bring in enough money to pay all the bills. However, if you have all your protocols and systems in place and are consistent in following them, then knowing the total number of patient visits you need to reach your goals can be crucial.

The numbers that are also very important are your Per Visit Revenue (PVR) and the amount of money you bring in per hour. PVR will tell you how much money each patient visit is worth. This will help you with your marketing budget. Let's say you're thinking of advertising on a billboard. The ad will cost you $3,000 and your PVR is $500. This means that you need to get at least six new patients as a result of that advertisement just to break even. In marketing, you need at least a 1:1.2 return to break even. In this case, your return should be at least $3,600 because there are hidden costs (such as paying staff for arranging the advertisement). Or if you do the work yourself, then you need to factor in the cost of your time away from seeing patients. If you don't think you can get six patients from the advertisement, then don't pull the trigger and place the ad.

If you're only concerned about filling your schedule, you can get in trouble. For example, if you didn't see many new patients and spent your day clipping toenails, even though you saw fifty patients, you'll soon realize that seeing *better quality* patients is more important.

For several reasons, it's extremely important to know how much money you're making per hour. First, you won't or shouldn't perform $10 per hour tasks when you can make between $600 and $700 per hour. Delegate these tasks to someone who is or can be trained to do them. Spending too much time on tasks that don't move the needle—meaning tasks that don't pay you more—is a surefire way to get burned out quickly.

Knowing your hourly worth will also help you think about ways to maximize each patient's services in order to increase your hourly wage. If you were making $400 an hour while seeing five patients, wouldn't it be better to see the same number of patients and make $650 an hour? Of course, it would, but how do you do this? You can add modalities like lasers for pain or nail fungus, or sell more custom orthotics to patients who will pay out of pocket, or add ancillary staff who can debride the nails and perform other lesser value services.

You can also figure out which type of patients are your best patients. The Pareto Principle states that 80 percent of the effects come from 20 percent of the causes. In this case, 80 percent of your income comes from 20 percent of your patients. So, who are your 20 percenters? Run a report in your EMR for the top 20 percent of all your diagnoses. If you see heel pain generates a big part of your income, then you should spend most of your marketing dollars promoting your services for heel pain.

The opposite is also true. Are you spending a lot of time and money on patients who have a certain diagnosis that doesn't bring a good return on your investment? I'm not saying that you shouldn't treat these people, but perhaps you could have allotted times to see these types of patients, rather than spending an entire day debriding nails. Try having Toenail Tuesday, where you see all these patients on Tuesday morning. If your state allows, have an assistant or some other ancillary staff person perform these procedures. But first figure out what your hourly wage is, so you can decide if you need to see more patients or simply work smarter with the volume you have.

:: ::

There are many other numbers to review, and as the CEO of your company, you should definitely do so. My purpose here isn't to overwhelm you, but to be complete. If you're already running weekly reports for the above numbers, then you're ready to graduate to the next level. Any time you run into a problem, you can usually figure out why you're having the problem by looking at the numbers.

Further, the numbers aren't just for you. In my practice, every staff member has a statistic they measure and analyze, which they report to me on a weekly basis. This is what we review each week at our staff meetings. The staff know that their graphs don't necessarily reflect on them as a worker, but they also know that the numbers help them know where to put their focus.

If you teach your staff how to analyze their own numbers, they'll take responsibility for their position and won't rely on you to tell them what they need to do all the time.

Let's look at each position in your practice and go over the graphs and statistics they need to keep and analyze.

Patient Care Coordinator

Your receptionist or patient care coordinator (PCC) actually has three jobs to accomplish on a daily basis.
- Make sure the patients keep their appointments.
- Keep the appointment book full of productive patients.
- Collect all monies that are due at the time of service and all past balances.

A productive patient is one that you can charge. You don't want to fill your day with post-ops or follow-ups. A productive patient is more than just an orthotic check-up; it's a patient to whom you'll deliver some sort of treatment. Of course, in order to complete those three tasks, the receptionist/patient care coordinator has a lot to do to accomplish these goals.

The PCC has three graphs to review and analyze each week. These graphs represent the percentage of patients that keep their appointments; the total number of patient visits per day, week, and month; and monies collected over the desk for the same time period.

You might wonder how he/she can get this done or why should he/she do this. I've consulted doctors who either did all the number crunching themselves or rarely looked at their numbers. The doctors who do it all themselves were spending way too much time in the office and weren't having enough fun time, and the ones who didn't look at their numbers don't have a clue about what's going on in their practice. You're an owner, thus you must think like one. You're the CEO of your organization, and you have to take full responsibility for everything that goes on in your practice.

Looking at the graph below, you can see the percentage of kept appointments over the last four weeks ranges from 94 percent to 100 percent. You want it to be at 95 percent or above. Ninety percent to 94 percent of kept appointments is good, but always strive for at least 95 percent.

It's not enough to say, "Hey, we're at 95 percent—fantastic! Keep up the great work everyone." You need to know what controls this number, and what factors affect the percentage of kept appointments. (By the way, most doctors don't analyze their numbers until they start to go down or even when the numbers have decreased over a longer period of time.)

Percentage of Kept Appointments

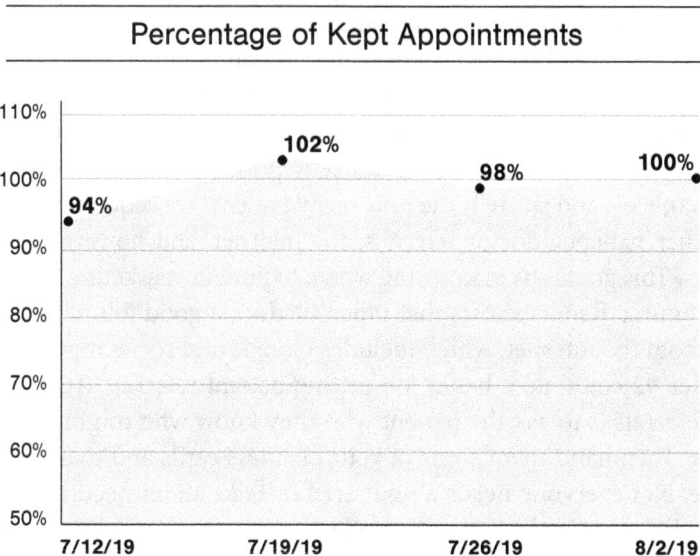

Your staff will be glad to take on the responsibility of making and analyzing the graphs because it gets them involved in the practice. They'll feel you trust them to make decisions based on the reports they run. But they need to know how to do it. I use Excel to make my graphs. I recommend that you run reports for all the graphs yourself for about four weeks, and after you get the hang of it, teach the staff how to do it. Write down the exact steps they need to perform for each report, and then show them how to make a graph. Once they learn how to do it, it will only take them a few minutes each week.

Marketing Director

If you have a marketer, then it's obvious that they're responsible for bringing in new patients. However, their job is also to communicate with current patients to make sure they come to you any time they have a foot or ankle problem.

You'll want to measure total number of patients who were recalled and made an appointment. We call and email all patients who haven't been seen in the past eight months. No single person makes these calls; we distribute them throughout the staff in order to get the job done.

When we make the call, our goal isn't to actually make an appointment, but to check in with the patient. We want to see how they're doing. We make some small talk and continue to develop the relationship. If they're not feeling 100 percent, we make an appointment with them. If they're doing great, we say, "I'm glad to hear that. If you or any of your friends or family need us, just let us know. We'll be here for you."

We also want to know where we are getting our patients, and my marketing director puts together a full Source Report. We have two charts—one for each office—and she tells me how many patients we acquired each week from other patients, doctor referrals, the internet, and however else they found us. This guides us in knowing where to put our marketing efforts.

The Source Report shows that office #1 does a good job of getting referrals from the internet, which includes Google and social media. We see that office #2 could do a better job getting patient referrals. The best way to get referrals is to ask the patient who they know who might need your services. Then hand them some of your business cards and thank them in advance. Not everyone needs a podiatrist or talks about needing one, but planting this seed in the patient's mind will cause them to think about who might need your services.

Source Report

Week of _____

SOURCE	# OF PATIENTS	SOURCE	# OF PATIENTS
Office #1		**Office #2**	
Patient	10	Patient	3
Website	8	Website	5
Email		Email	
L&L/Event		L&L/Event	
Mailer		Mailer	
Yellow Pages		Yellow Pages	
Internet	12	Internet	7
Amazon		Amazon	
Groupon		Groupon	2
Google	12	Google	
YouTube		YouTube	
Doctor	9	Doctor	4
Been here before	3	Been here before	3
Rutgers		Rutgers	1
Insurance book	2	Insurance book	1
Employee		Employee	
N/A Walk in	1	N/A Walk in	1
Signs		Signs	
Event		Event	
Ad	1	Ad	
TOTAL	58	**TOTAL**	26

Financial Administrator

The purpose of the financial administrator is to collect your money, not to simply bill for your services. A lot of doctors call this person the biller. They even put advertisements out for a biller. You *do not* want a biller. You want a *collector*. A collector is great at billing, but they also follow up with the insurances and patients for all monies that are due. If you find someone who can be nice and develop rapport with people while having the ability to get them to pay, then you have struck gold, my friend. Do whatever you need to do to keep him or her.

KPIs for the financial administrator:
- Total collections weekly, monthly, and yearly
- Accounts receivable for insurances and patients
- Clean claims rate
- Total number of collection calls to patients and insurance companies with promises to pay

We do our billing in house, but even if you do it offsite, you still want the following information. Each week, our financial department gives me our total weekly collections and our accounts receivable. Regarding the A/R, they make a graph for all monies due by patients and insurances.

I receive a graph that shows monies owed that are in the 0- to 30-day bucket and another graph for anything over thirty days. I want to see the A/R go down for anything that is older than thirty days, but it can be good if the 0- to 30-day bucket is going up because it means we're producing, and a decent amount of money should be coming in really soon. If our A/R is going up, I want to know why. What are we doing or not doing?

A/R	0–30	31–60	61–90	91–120	121–150	151–179	180>
Insurance	$189,753	$34,357	$12,977	$12,665	$2,216	$2,101	$7,959
Patients	$8,471	$6,879	$1,932	$2,707	$677	$870	$5,197
Total	**$198,224**	**$41,236**	**$14,909**	**$15,372**	**$2,893**	**$2,971**	**$13,156**

Sometimes monies are on the A/R report that shouldn't be because we'll never collect it. For example, you may get paid for a certain surgery and ask the insurance company to review the claim for additional payment. Then you get a second denial but don't remove the remaining balance from the A/R. This gives the false impression that the A/R is high.

There's another number that I track that most people don't. It's the *number of collection calls* made per week to insurance companies and to patients, respectively. How did I come up with this? Just like most everything else, I reverse engineered it. How do you tackle your A/R? The only way is to call people. Most doctors only send statements. Sending statements not only costs you money, but it isn't effective. When people have more month than money, they have to decide who gets paid. Of course, the mortgage or rent gets paid first, then the car, the phone, gas and electric, and water bills will all be paid before the doctor. Your job is to be next in line. The squeaky wheel gets the grease, as they say. So, send your statement but also follow up with phone calls.

When my financial team makes a total of one hundred patient calls and one hundred insurance calls per week, I see an increase in my collections. Let me clarify: these are productive calls that get commitments from the insurance companies and individuals. If I outsourced my billing, I'd want to see a weekly list of claims that were called on and the results of those calls. Outsourcing is good, but it doesn't give you permission to forgo your responsibility for your bottom line. Don't be afraid to be a pest to your billing company. It's your money, your business, and your life. You have the right to know what's going on in your business.

Medical Assistants

The medical assistant's job is to expedite patient care and allow you to move from treatment room to treatment room without a hitch. You shouldn't have to leave the room to retrieve items or to look for people. This slows you down, and if you have thirty patients in a day and you run two minutes behind for each patient, then you'll be behind by one hour by the end of the day. The assistant's job is to make sure the treatment rooms are fully stocked with supplies. They also help market the practice.

By the way, all our staff members wear two hats. One hat is their main job, like the financial person, the PCC, etc., and the second hat is the marketer hat. In the treatment room, if the assistant finds out the patient is really happy with their care, he/she asks if they know anyone else with a foot or ankle problem. If they do, the assistant gives them a referral packet that contains information about our practice and the doctors, a magnet, a pedicure file with our logo on it, history forms, and a pamphlet explaining the potential patient's foot problem. This packet is oversized to prevent the patient from putting it in his/her purse and forgetting it. We write the potential patient's name on the front of the packet to personalize it. Then we measure the number of referral packets that we hand out.

We also measure our on-time percentages—the number of the patients who were brought into the room at their appointment time. If the rooms are fully stocked and the doctor doesn't dawdle, then patients should be brought in on time (of course, we can't control when the patient is late). Each assistant carries the daily schedule with them at all times. They know that if the patient is scheduled for 10:00 a.m., then they need to be in the room right at 10:00. If it's a new patient who didn't fill out the forms prior to their appointment, then we understand that the patient won't be brought back right on time. We expect new patients to be in the room within fifteen minutes of their appointment. The assistant marks an X on the paper schedule if they're not in the room on time, or they record a check mark if they are.

There are a lot of reasons that could cause a patient not to be brought into the treatment room on time. The purpose of the on-time graph is to start a conversation and handle the problems we can control, which we discuss at our weekly meeting. We strive for 95 percent or better. If it falls below 90 percent, then we need to correct it immediately—but the whole point of graphing and analyzing statistics is to prevent us from going into panic mode. If we're normally at 95 percent and it goes down to 93 percent, I ask why. If you think 93 percent isn't bad and you ignore it, then the next thing you'll see is that number going down to 88 percent. Find out the reason for the slight dip before it becomes a problem. In this case, the problem could be that your patients were upset that they had to wait too long, and they wrote a negative review.

Practice Administrator

How do you measure the role of an administrator or office manager? Their job is to oversee the overall office, and the goal is to make sure that everyone else is meeting their goals. We measure seven key numbers, and our PAL's goal is to achieve at least five of them. The administrator is your on-the-floor cheerleader and coach. They organize the daily game plan and help each staff member to focus on their number one priority for the day. They stop the unnecessary chatter and cheer the team on when they're doing well. They basically motivate everyone to keep on doing a great job and make sure they don't take their foot off the gas pedal.

But how do you measure this? If the goal is to get everyone to achieve their goals, then the KPI is the number of statistics that are trending upward. Take a look at the PAL graph and chart. There are seven KPIs: collections, new patients, visits, percentage kept appointments, percentage of patients brought into the room on time, number of patients who were called to come back to the office (recalls), and charges. The administrator looks at this graph to see what areas need focus during the upcoming week. It's very difficult to focus on everything, so the idea is to find *the one thing* that affects everything else.

This chart shows that the only goal that wasn't met was for collections. However, since new patients, visits, and charges all trended up, then collections should be rolling in. The administrator needs to make sure that the financial department is on top of calling on the A/R, especially the

PAL Graph # Stats >/= Above (7)

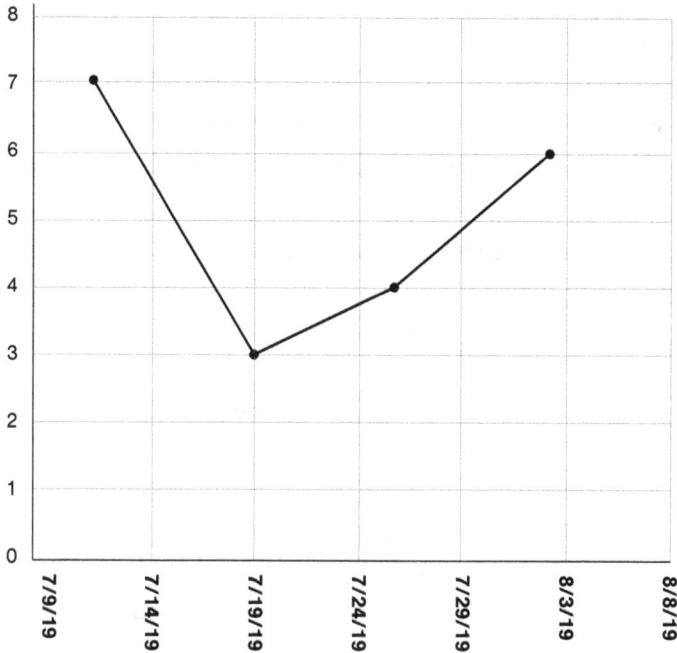

ACTUAL	PREVIOUS WK	CURRENT WK	GOAL
Collections	44,783	46,612	47,917
NP	48	64	48
Visits	290	325	313
%Kept	101	101	90
%On Time	96	96	90
Recalls	146	128	100
Charges	91,837	89,722	85,835

big-ticket items that are less than ninety days old. In addition, collections should be coming in during the next two weeks from this week's charges. Next, the PAL would focus on getting new patients scheduled immediately in order to continue the upward trend.

Other Key Numbers:

- Amount of money collected over the desk: This tells you if your staff is collecting all monies due at the time of service, as well as past balances.

- Percentage of money collected per day: Review your schedule and add up the total amount of money that should be collected, which includes past balances and co-pays for the day's services. At the end of the day, see how much you actually collected and calculate the percentage. You can't predict what patients will owe for their deductibles, but it helps you get an idea if your front desk is on top of things.

- Total visits: You want your appointment book full of productive patients.

- Total accounts receivable: This number shouldn't be more than two months' gross billing.

- Total accounts aging, greater than ninety days: Should be less than 15 percent of total A/R.

- Clean claim rate: Should be higher than 97 percent.

- Payroll ratio: Should be between 22 percent and 26 percent. This includes staff benefits but excludes all DPMs. The exception is the very busy practice that has several ancillary staff who provide services throughout the day, such as laser therapy, debridement of nails, and any treatment that is financially lucrative. In these practices, the ratio can go up to 30 percent.

- New patients: Should be between 15 percent and 20 percent of total patient volume.

- Marketing budget: Should be approximately 5 to 10 percent of the total budget. That number doesn't include the marketing director's salary. Including the salary, it should be around 14 to 15 percent.

- Days in receivable: Equals average A/R divided by gross annual charges x 360. This should be no more than forty-five to fifty days.

- Days in inventory: Equals average inventory divided by annual cost x 360. It should be not more than sixty days. This doesn't include any promotional items.

Analyzing Your Numbers

Simply running reports and putting numbers in a graph doesn't do anything except give you a number. The trick is to figure out what these numbers mean and to know what action to take as a result of knowing these numbers. I've spent a lot of time compiling a list of actions that will cause each number in your practice to either go up or down. In this section, I'll teach you how to look at a graph and make good decisions about what you need to do in order to improve that specific statistic.

A Word about Graphs

When you look at your graphs, you'll want to compare the previous two weeks, even though a trend is measured over four weeks. Graphs, if not analyzed properly, will give you false data, and they can make things appear to be good even when they aren't. On the contrary, you can look at the graph and decide your practice is in trouble, but when you sit down and analyze the situation, you might find it really isn't so bad. If a particular graph trended up over the last week, but overall it's still less than it normally has been, then you need to find out what caused the slight increase. But what's more important is to figure out what caused the numbers to go down during that three-week period and correct it. A slight increase can fool you into thinking you've solved the problem. If the numbers keep going up over the next few weeks, then you probably corrected the problem and can continue to focus and strengthen the situation.

In short, you not only need to make decisions about what occurred over the last week, but about what happened over a four-week trend. One good week doesn't solve the problem, and one little blip isn't a reason to call a bankruptcy attorney.

You not only need to make decisions about
what occurred over the last week, but about what
happened over a four-week trend.

Production

Production = your charges. Look at the following graph. It shows a downward trend over the last four weeks, and you need to determine—with your team—what caused it.

Production is certainly affected by the number of new patients and total visits. But what else can affect production?

- Promoting your services
- Efficient medical assistants
- Percentage of patient appointments kept
- Proper scheduling

- New patient visits
- Well-stocked treatment rooms
- Following treatment protocols
- Making patients feel comfortable
- Verifying insurance benefits
- Following your recall system
- Scheduling tests
- Informing doctors about missed or cancelled appointments
- Proper coding
- Smiling
- Insurance participation
- Properly stocked inventory
- Patient referrals

Production

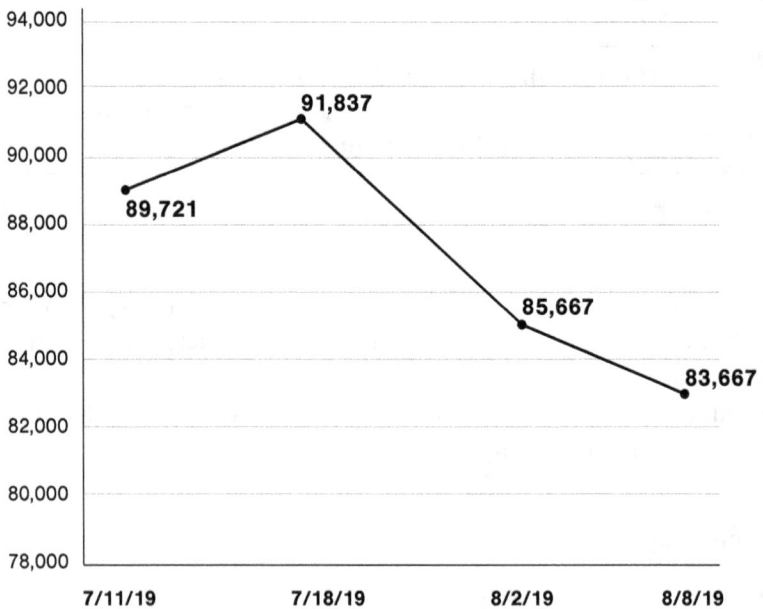

So how else could you handle a falling production problem? The first thing to do is promote your services. Perhaps you stopped a certain marketing campaign or stopped visiting doctors in the neighborhood. It could mean you took too many days off. That's definitely okay to do, as long as you plan on making it up in the weeks to come or if you're okay with having this temporary dip in your numbers. It could also mean that you're exhausted and you're working way too hard, and you need to find a way to rejuvenate yourself.

The graphs are there to guide you. After you discover why your numbers are decreasing, you need to take action. If action means you need to increase your marketing and find a way to provide all the necessary services to the patient at the time of service, then that's what you need to do. Next, involve your team and delegate the tasks. If you simply don't have the manpower, then your numbers may dip because of that—so go out and get your next "A" team player! The bottom line is to take immediate action before the problem becomes too serious.

Proper scheduling is one area that affects production. If you schedule a lot of follow-ups or post-ops in one day, then your production will suffer. Try to spread these appointments around if possible. Not having enough supplies will certainly affect your production, so make sure you keep track of your inventory.

Also, on the list is insurance participation, but not accepting certain insurances is sometimes a good thing. If the insurance company reimburses poorly, you don't have to accept it. Even though you might not be able to see these patients anymore—which could cause a decrease in your short-term production—your collections could increase, which is the main thing you want. If you don't accept poor-paying insurances, you can schedule patients who have better insurances, which will increase your bottom line. Or better yet, introduce more cash services to the practice.

Percentage of Kept Appointments

When it comes to percentages, each graph is analyzed differently. For example, for percent of kept appointments, you're aiming for anything equal to or higher than 95 percent. However, it's still considered good if your percentage is between 90 percent and 94 percent. You just don't want anything below 90 percent. It doesn't mean that you should accept 92 percent, it just means you might need a little tweak here or there, or simply remind the staff and doctors to make sure patients understand why they need to come in for their next visit. With any of these statistics, just being aware of something is often enough.

Percentage of Kept Appointments

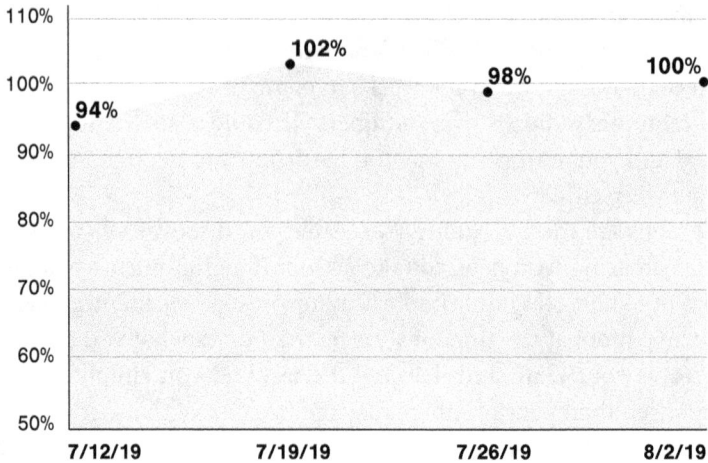

What Affects Percentage of Kept Appointments:
- Being on time
- Friendly and prompt service on the phone
- Educating patients about why they need to return
- Convenient office hours
- Staff's ability to answer the patient's questions
- Customer service
- Cost of services, deductibles, and co-pays
- The patient's fear of pain
- The patient's fear of the unknown
- Flexible scheduling
- Developing rapport with the patient
- Proper phone etiquette
- Having a clean and modern office
- Modern technology
- Not using lay terms to educate the patient
- Lack of quality time spent with the patient
- Lack of empathy

Be tuned in to the patient and respond to what they want and need. Nobody likes to wait when they've a scheduled an appointment with you. Patients are concerned about fear of pain and the unknown, the cost of the treatment, and they need to understand the purpose of their next appointment, and how many appointments it usually takes to get rid of their problem.

I've interviewed many doctors for an associate position, and during the interview I always ask, "How do you treat heel pain?" Many times, they'll say that they tape the foot and prescribe an anti-inflammatory. That's it. No injections and no night splints. Many patients have high co-pays or deductibles, and let me tell you, when the tape falls off in one or two days, and the patient paid a $50 co-pay, guess what? You have a very angry patient.

Your job is to get the patient better quickly. Piecemealing the treatment process can be very expensive for them. If they decide they don't want to try everything at once, that's fine. You did your job when you explained what and why you want to perform certain treatments and told them it can be more expensive if you do only one thing at a time.

When a patient cancels an appointment, make sure your staff knows that you have an empty slot in the schedule. The patient care coordinator's job is to keep the schedule full of productive patients, so they should try to get the next patient who calls for an appointment to come in that day. They can make it sound like the patient hit the jackpot. "Mrs. Jones, you're in luck, our 2:30 slot just opened up. We can get you in today and get you better right away. How does that sound?"

The PCC can also call any patient who's been trying to get in but hasn't been able to. If your office schedule gets booked really quickly, then you should already have a list of patients that need to be scheduled. Also take a look at the people who didn't show up or cancelled an appointment in the last couple of weeks and give them a call. Maybe you have a list of patients who need to pick up their orthotics, shoes, or braces. Offer them that empty slot. Providing exceptional service is the best way to make sure your patients keep returning, and there's no reason for staff to be sitting around doing nothing.

Collections

Reviewing your collections is critical. In fact, I review this number every day, because then I can make sure that we're consistent in our production.

Take a look at the at the Collections Weekly graph, which indicates a slight increase in collections over the past three weeks. However, you'll also notice that it's down slightly from the number four weeks ago.

Collections Weekly

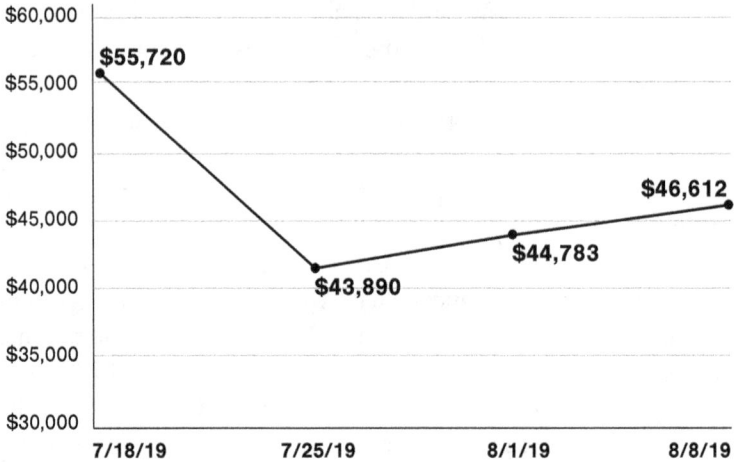

The first question to ask is if $55,720 is an outlier. Have you ever collected that much before? If you normally collect amounts around this number, then why has there been a decrease in your collections? The good news is that the money is slowly creeping up. But if you need to collect $50,000 per week to pay yourself and your vendors, then you're not out of the woods.

What Affects Collections:

- New patients
- Ability to sell your services
- Verifying benefits prior to treatment
- A/R and collecting
- Proper coding
- Patients keeping their appointments
- Informing patients about costs prior to treatment
- Financial policies enforced
- Gathering proper patient demographic information
- Electronic claims submission
- Timely filing of claims
- Getting referrals
- Collecting all monies due at time of service

- Proper data entry
- Timely follow-ups with insurances and patients who owe money
- Making calls regarding A/R in addition to sending statements
- Clean claims
- Smiling

Doctors who have outside billing services have less control over this statistic than those who do onsite billing. Many billing companies don't provide you with all the information, and when you ask for it, they don't respond in a timely fashion. This is your business, and you need to know what's going on at any given time of the day. If you can't sleep (and the whole purpose of this book is to make sure you sleep well), and you want to know how much money you're bringing in this month, then even if it's 2:30 a.m., you want to be able to access this information.

Further, if the reason why your collections are declining is due to your collection team, then you can sit down with them and go over the possible causes. Is your team calling on the A/R? Are they calling patients for past-due balances in addition to sending them statements? Are the claims going out cleanly in a timely fashion? Is your front desk collecting all co-pays and deductibles at the time of service? Are orthotics distributed without getting paid from either the insurance companies or the patient themselves?

Humor me for a moment while I touch on the subject of smiling. Everything and everyone in your office responds to smiling. Smiling is so powerful. Why does it affect your collections? When you smile, it shows confidence and makes other people happy.

People who feel good are more likely to pay. After paying their mandatory monthly bills, the patient has to decide which other bills to pay, especially if he or she doesn't have enough money to pay them all. Their decision to pay you is based on whether they like you or not. If they like you better than the other doctor, then you're more likely to get paid.

So, building rapport is very important. If you have a nasty receptionist, then there's an increased likelihood that the patient won't want to pay just on principle. Asking for money isn't easy, but doing so with confidence and pleasantries goes a long way.

New Patients

We have a saying in podiatry: *Treat them and street them.* We get our patients better quickly and then they're done, unless they have a new problem. We live and die by the number of new patients we see. The number of new patients you see is where you must focus. It's the keystone of all your metrics. When you increase your number of new patients, your production and collections will increase, too. Further, if your marketing focuses on the key diagnoses that bring in the biggest dollars, then your per visit revenue will grow even higher.

New Patients Weekly

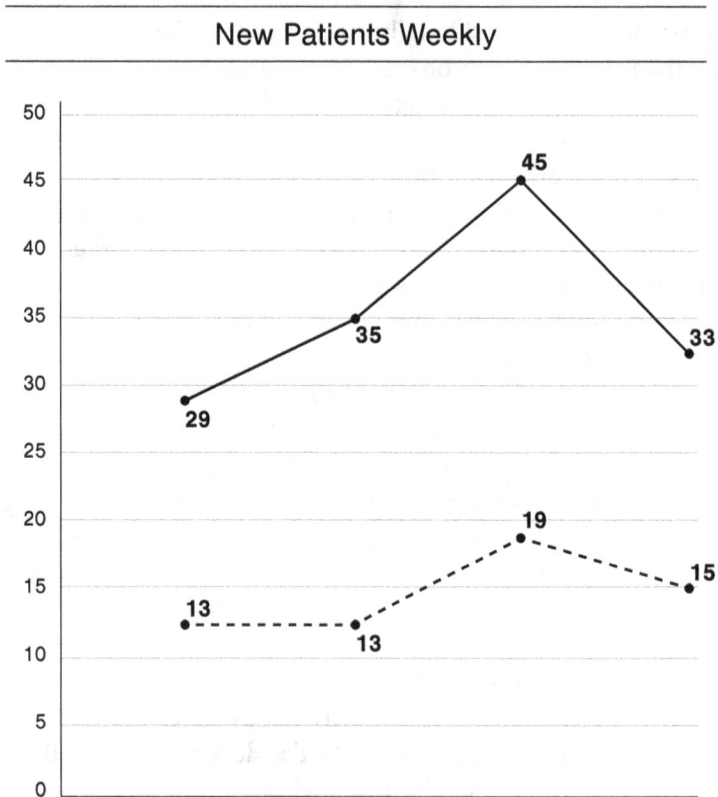

	7/26/19	8/2/19	8/9/19	8/16/19
—— Office #1	29	35	45	33
- - - Office #2	13	13	19	15

The graph reflects the number of new patients we saw weekly in each office. Both offices experienced a decline from the previous week, but over the last four weeks, the new patients number remained steady. In both offices, the prior week was above the normal for our practice. However, if we reached that number once, why can't we achieve it every week? The trick is to dig deep and find out what caused that number to rise.

> ### We live and die by the number of new patients we see.

What Affects New Patients:

- Phone etiquette
- Staying on time
- Letters and phone calls to referring doctors
- Letters and gifts to patients who refer others
- An updated website
- Excellent reviews
- A clean and modern office
- Selling your services
- Accepting insurance
- Marketing to partners who will refer you
- Excellent communication between staff and patients
- Delivering on your promises
- Returning patient phone calls
- Patient education literature
- Following phone scenarios
- Marketing new procedures
- Modern technology
- Office signage
- Staff and doctor who smile
- Lunch and Learn programs
- Making things convenient for the patient
- Handing out referral cards and packets
- Refrigerator magnets
- Newsletters to patients
- Newsletters to other physicians
- Social media posts
- A clean and modern office

- Conducting seminars and participating in health fairs
- Patient surveys

Earlier, I mentioned that we give out referral cards and packets that are personalized with the potential patient's name. We offer the new patient a free examination (treatment and X-rays not included). You can't do this in every state, so please consult your own state laws. We put an expiration date on this offer, which gives it a sense of urgency. When the new patient comes in, we send the referring patient a gift, like an office mug with our logo on it. The gift is a total surprise and a gesture of gratitude.

We also like to stay in front of our referring physicians, so we have Lunch and Learn programs at their office, which is usually more *lunch* than *learn*. The programs are always scheduled, and we're usually only in their office for about fifteen minutes. We also send them a physician newsletter—only one page—that talks about a new procedure, or a case study, or how we treat certain foot or ankle problems. The reason drug reps keep coming to your office is because they know that when they show up, you write more prescriptions for their drug. The same is true for referring doctors. When you keep your name in front of them, they're more likely to refer to you over the podiatrist down the street.

Other Indicators

There are other numbers and graphs that can help you get a real picture of your practice. Let's say your production is up, collections are down, new patients are up, but total visits for that week are down.

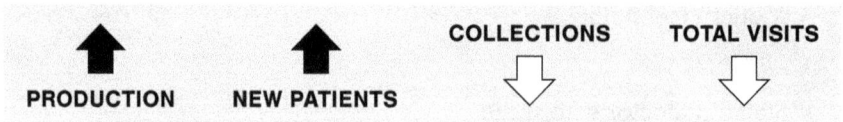

⬆ PRODUCTION   ⬆ NEW PATIENTS   COLLECTIONS ⬇   TOTAL VISITS ⬇

In this example, you'd think that your collections would be up because both production and new patients were up. So why did your collections and total visits go down? My first question would be this: Are your new patients returning? Check to see if the new patients made their next appointment, and if they did, did they cancel it or not show up? If that's the case, you need to get a handle on it. Your staff needs to call them to find out why they missed their appointment and try to get them back in.

If you're charging more but collecting less, then find out if there's resistance to paying at the time of service. Perhaps you performed a lot of procedures and you're still waiting for payment. If so, then keep a close watch on your collections for the next few weeks.

Another reason these numbers could be skewed is that your new patients aren't productive ones. Perhaps you saw a lot of patients who needed to have their toenails debrided.

Don't look at only one number. You need to look at all your numbers to give you the full picture of how healthy your practice is.

Everyone's Accountable

You must continually have your finger on the pulse of your business. Every week, all my staff members complete their graphs and email them to me on Friday afternoon. First, they analyze their graphs and explain why their numbers went up or down, then provide an action plan for the upcoming week. It's important to plan a specific, dedicated time in your day to review and analyze these numbers and graphs. I do it on Fridays after I receive my team's emails. It only takes about fifteen minutes because I've trained my staff to analyze the numbers themselves. Because I'd previously set up the formulas and graphs in Excel spreadsheets, all they have to do is plug in the numbers.

We discuss each of their graphs during our Monday meeting that all staff attends. During that meeting, we also finalize the plans for that week. This is why I don't need to micromanage my team anymore. The numbers tell me what I need to know.

Focusing on your numbers on a daily, weekly, and quarterly basis can be overwhelming at first, but trust me, it's well worth the time when you understand the process. The purpose of knowing your numbers is to identify the areas of your practice that need focus, so you can attain your personal financial and life goals. Your practice is meant to serve you, so why not make every area of it shine?

CHAPTER 9:

Get Your Patients to Say Yes

"Approach each customer with the idea of helping him or her to solve a problem or achieve a goal, not of selling a product or service."
– Brian Tracy

Selling: it's a word a lot of people disdain, especially doctors. It conjures up images of a used car salesman who hounds someone until they buy from them. Just thinking about sales can give you a bad feeling if you think that selling means trying to get someone to do something they don't want to do—as if it's a form of trickery

But it's not. The definition of sales is to *give people what they need or want at the right time and at the right price.* The right time means that you don't pitch the patient to have bunion surgery immediately if their daughter is getting married next week, or you don't sell expensive orthotics to an elderly patient who rarely walks.

We all sell, and you already have plenty of experience doing it. For example, when you went on a date, you first had to sell yourself to the other person. You had to put on the extra big smile, comb and quaff your hair, freshen your breath, and pick the right time to ask that girl or guy out. That's definitely selling. When you went on interviews, you had to sell yourself to the prospective employer, and now you're selling yourself to every patient, hoping to earn their trust. You are always selling, even if you don't realize it.

If it's done right, neither you nor the patient will feel like you're selling. Further, the patient will be more inclined to accept your treatment proposals. Why? Because selling is simply showing how much you care. In my opinion, it's easy for doctors to sell. We have the knowledge and experience, and even Dr. Google can't claim that. But there are many patients who don't accept our treatment plans or simply give us a hard time. How can you get patients to listen to you and accept your recommendations?

The first step is to display confidence in yourself and your skills. On the initial visit, the patient doesn't know you and doesn't know if she can trust you. A nice, warm smile and a firm handshake will help break the ice. Don't be overly enthusiastic. You want to match the patient's tone. If they're nervous or depressed, show some understanding and try to put them at ease.

The point is to establish a relationship. Next, make great eye contact. When you make eye contact, the patient will feel you're listening.

Now you need to ask great questions and listen with intent. Find out the one thing they can't do, or what they wish they could do, without experiencing pain. What keeps them up at night? What are their fears?

Someone might come to see you for bunion pain, which they've put off for months or even years because they're afraid. They're afraid they'll need surgery, afraid that if they have surgery they could be crippled for life, or afraid of disfigurement—meaning that their foot will be ugly after surgery. These fears are often fed by their friends and relatives. "Oh, my friend had that done. She was in tremendous pain afterwards and still can't walk without pain and she had it done two years ago." The person who said this to your patient may have meant well, but that doesn't help your cause.

Today, patients can view any procedure online thanks to YouTube. I tell my patients to stay off chat sites and not to watch online videos. What we do in the operating room is fun to us, but to most people, it looks pretty scary.

Address Three Things First

The first three things you must address are time, fear, and money.

The first three things you must address are time, fear, and money.

A patient might say, "I don't have time to come to see you," or, "I don't have time to get the surgery or go to physical therapy or to get the laser treatment." If he is afraid, he's probably concerned about whether it will hurt and what he will be able to do afterward. "Will I be able to play sports again?" or, "Will I be able to walk normally and do all the things I did before?"

Patient: "Will I be able to play the piano after the surgery?"

Doctor: "I don't see why not."

Patient: "That's funny. I wasn't able to play it before."

That's a very old joke, but I couldn't resist!

And, of course, your patient will be concerned about the costs. Will his insurance cover the costs, or will he/she have to pay out of pocket?

Time

First of all, you have to have convenient hours if you're going to provide a series of treatments. For example, each laser session only takes ten minutes, and it doesn't take many treatments to get better. And, doctor, be sure that you are on time for each appointment. Patients will cancel their appointments or refuse to come back if you make them wait. It's disrespectful to them and their own full calendar.

When it comes to selling surgery and the expected downtime afterward, don't sugarcoat it. Tell the patient why they need the procedure and what can happen if they don't have it. Be honest and straightforward regarding outcomes and expectations. Tell them about the downtime during recovery and their limitations during that time, and tell them when they can get back to their regular activities. If the patient will be in a walking boot for four weeks, then that's what it is. Tell it to them straight. Patients get upset if you aren't honest with them.

If the patient is concerned about his time, you can also offer him alternative procedures. If he can't come in every two weeks for four to five visits—for heel pain, for example—you can give him an injection, a night splint, and make his orthotics all in the same visit. If his insurance won't cover multiple products dispensed on the same day, explain the situation and tell him he can pay out of pocket for the orthotics or splint.

He might object, but convenience comes at a cost. You can put a rush on any order, but there's usually an additional fee. Overnight delivery costs more, too. When someone values time over money, then they'll pay more to save time.

Another alternative could be high energy ESWT treatment or cryosurgery, which has no downtime. You can be creative in order to help your patient, as long as what you recommend will treat the problem and the treatment is ethical.

Fear

We start mitigating fear with the first phone call. Before anything, you—and your staff, who are an extension of you—must develop rapport with the patient. When your staff answers the phone, make it a warm welcome, like, "Welcome to Family Foot & Ankle Specialists. This is Ashley speaking. How may I help you?" They should repeat the patient's name three times during the conversation.

Here's a key question your staff can ask the patient: "What seems to be bothering you?" After the patient answers, your staff member should express empathy by saying something like, "Oh, that seems painful. You've called the right place. We can definitely help you with that. Our doctors see that all the time and they're very gentle."

This exchange will help to relax the potential patient. They're telling the patient that they called the right place because the doctors can take care of the problem. When they hear that you see their condition all the time, the patient feels relieved that they don't have something weird going on—it's a common problem the doctors can handle. The clincher is to say that the doctors are very gentle, which helps calm their fear of pain.

When they come to see you and you present the treatment options, don't paint a bleak picture or sound depressing. Always lead with energy. Smile to show that you're confident. If you say they need an injection, understand that the patient might be afraid. Always come from a place of love and understanding, and say something soothing like this: "Mrs. Jones, I'm going to give you a steroid injection. A steroid is an anti-inflammatory that will help reduce the swelling of the tendon and help with your pain. The key is to get the swelling down as soon as possible. First, I'll apply a cold spray to numb the skin, and the injection will only take five seconds. You'll be able to perform all of your activities that you normally do."

During this presentation, look at your patient. Don't ask her if she wants an injection; no one wants an injection. What she wants is to be pain free.

I don't always go into this full presentation with every patient. I can tell if I need to calm them by considering their body language and noticing their facial expressions. If they seem okay with it, I proceed without the chat.

Sometimes patients try to hide their fears by saying things like, "Will my insurance cover it?" Or, "I don't want to mask the pain," or, "I hear steroids are bad for you." You should address these issues, but remember that the underlying reason may be that they're afraid of the pain.

If a patient objects to having an injection, I say: "Mrs. Jones, do you know how to build a fire? First you put in the kindling—the small branches or paper. When you light it, it causes a small flame. After that, you can put on the big log. An injection is like the kindling. It starts the treatment process. Next, we'll be able to make you custom inserts to prevent the problem from recurring. The injection allows the other treatments to work even better."

Money

When it comes to dealing with money, doctors seem to have a hard time. During the initial phone call, we ask the patient for their insurance information but, of course, it's not the first thing we ask. It's really important to develop rapport with the patient, and you can't do that if the first thing out of your mouth is about their insurance. We accept most insurances, and our financial team verifies the benefits prior to the patient's visit. If the patient didn't have the insurance information when they first called, we set up a convenient time to call them back to get that information.

When they arrive for their appointment, explain their benefits and approximately what they'll owe prior to treatment. Patients get upset if they receive an unexpected bill in the mail. Nobody wants to buy something without first knowing the price. What they want and deserve is the right to make their own decisions regarding their health and their finances. Discuss the costs up front.

If a patient calls for an appointment and you either don't accept their insurance or they don't have insurance, we offer them a free initial exam. We explain that X-rays and treatment are not included, but when we determine the problem, we'll discuss the cost of the treatment plan. The goal is to get them into the office to meet you. But be warned: the free exam program only works if you have a great staff and you provide great service. If your staff is nasty or just plain rude, there's no way a patient will pay you.

There are several ways to handle money in the treatment room. A lot of doctors separate the medical side from the business side. In most cases, I agree with this approach, and it all depends on how comfortable you are when discussing money. The main concern is the patient's well-being.

When you're in the treatment room, you need to be 100 percent focused on helping the patient. Once you get agreement on the treatment plan, you can have a staff member go in and discuss costs and payment. If it's simply explaining the cost of non-covered services, like orthotics or laser treatments, then you can do it yourself or not. The positive side of handling this yourself is that the patient doesn't have to wait for someone else to come in, and you're probably better at answering questions the patient might have about the treatment. The downside is that you might not be good at explaining costs and discussing payment options, or you simply feel uncomfortable because you don't want to come across as a salesman.

If you want a staff member to discuss the costs, first be sure the patient completely understands the treatment plan you've recommended. If the patient isn't convinced that they want the treatment—or if they don't fully understand it—it's unlikely that they'll accept the plan from someone else.

Be sure the right person presents the costs. Your financial person doesn't necessarily understand the patient's medical problem, which is why I have my medical assistant, who's thoroughly trained to discuss finances, present the costs to the patient. Our medical assistants have great knowledge of what we do, plus they can honestly convey the results that they've seen in similar situations. The key is to train them how to explain the finances.

However you decide to approach it, be sure to do what's comfortable for you to handle the three roadblocks to buying: time, fear, and money.

Confidence in Your Products

Doctors may balk at selling because they aren't totally confident in the product. Orthotics are a big part of podiatry practices and provide a lot of revenue. And yet, there are still a lot of podiatrists who have a problem recommending them to their patients. My consulting clients tell me that they don't think everyone needs orthotics or that they don't believe custom orthotics work any better than the over-the-counter ones. I'm not here to convince you about the importance of orthotics or the efficacy of the product, but I can tell you that if you don't believe in them, then you won't recommend them.

I'm a graduate of the school of biomechanics (CCPM—California College of Podiatric Medicine—now Samuel Merritt), and I'm blessed to have been trained by Dr. John Weed, Dr. Paul Scherer, Dr. Jack Morris, and Dr. Chris Smith. At CCPM, we made every pair of orthotics we casted ourselves. We learned what to do when orthotics don't work or don't feel good.

I'm able to modify every orthotic in my office. I believe the most common reasons that doctors don't believe in their orthotics or don't prescribe enough of them is because (a) they don't know what to do when the patient says that they hurt, and (b) the art of biomechanics is slowly dying and doctors don't know how to prescribe them. So, they prescribe the same type for almost every patient.

How do you answer a patient when they ask you the difference between an orthopedist who operates on the foot and you, the podiatrist? I tell them that we understand the biomechanics of the foot, and when we operate, we think of the foot's function, not just the aesthetics. There are many courses you can take to brush up on your biomechanics and orthotic prescribing. Unfortunately, we spent three years in residency learning surgery and wound care, but we hardly spent any time watching someone walk.

Here's a script for treating patients with heel pain to convince them to accept your recommendations:

First Heel Pain Visit

1. Greet the patient with a handshake and a warm smile and say your name slowly. Tell them it's a pleasure to meet them. Ask if they had any difficulty finding your office.

2. Get a complete history and find out what they can't do because of the pain. Find out how the pain affects their lives. Ask them to rate their pain on a scale from 1-10, with 10 being the worst.

3. Always look them in the eye and be confident. Speak slowly and in layman's terms.

How to explain the cause of their heel spur or plantar fasciitis: Dr: (looking at the X-rays in front of the patient). "Mrs. Jones, I will explain everything to you from the drawing board. We all have a tendon (I use the term tendon because most people don't understand what a ligament or fascia is) that goes from the heel bone to the ball of the foot." (Now draw the tendon on the board. It's important to use visuals, especially today, since most people are very visual.)

Next, show her the plantar fascia on their foot. Move the big toe back and gently rub your thumb on the fascia. Then say: "This is the band of tendon I'm talking about. When you walk, this tendon pulls harder than it normally should. When it pulls harder, it gets swollen or inflamed." I write two words on the board: Pulling and Inflamed. "The pain is from excessive pulling of the tendon on the heel bone. Due to the excessive pressure, the tendon becomes swollen or inflamed."

If she has a spur, I say: "As the tendon keeps pulling, it irritates the bone. The bone wants to protect itself, so it lays down calcium in the direction of the pull. This is called a spur. It's just like when you hold a pen tightly, and it causes a callous to be formed. The spur never causes pain. It's the inflamed ligament that causes the pain. This condition is called plantar fasciitis, and the reason I'm giving you this $25 word is because you might want to look it up on our website when you get home."

At this point, ask her if she understands everything you've explained. If she has morning pain, bring out the foot model and tell her to pretend there's a rubber band that goes from the heel bone to the ball of the foot. Demonstrate that when you move the heel through eversion, the arch collapses and causes this ligament to overstretch. Explain: "At night while your foot is at rest, the ligament is relaxed and shortened. The shortening causes the tendon to be tight, thus causing pain when you try to stretch it out with the first step in the morning. When you walk for a while, the tendon usually stretches out, and the pain will go away. It will recur if you're on your feet for long."

Ask her if this makes sense. Throughout your presentation, ask her questions that will likely cause her to say yes. This will help in the closing.

Remember that you began the visit by asking how the pain affected her daily activity. Now you can say: "Let me tell you how we're going to get you back on your feet, so you can run again. How does that sound?" This is a very important question and gets them nodding yes.

"First, we'll get a diagnostic ultrasound to see how inflamed the tendon is. This will help us during the treatment process." Get the ultrasound and show her the thickness of the plantar fascia. "The plantar fascia is normally between .35-.40 cm thick. Your tendon measures .68 cm, which is almost twice the normal size. To make this better, we have to stop the tendon from pulling and reduce the inflammation (point to the board). I'll stop the inflammation by injecting an anti-inflammatory medication mixed with an anesthetic. The medication is a steroid, but it won't make you run faster or hit a baseball like Barry Bonds."

It's good to joke with them. Have fun with the patients. Smile; it shows confidence. You're not selling them the treatment, you're selling yourself.

"After that, I'll tape your foot to stop the tendon from pulling. This will put your foot in a new position, which is very comfortable and will help the tendon to relax. In three days, you'll remove the tape and wear the arch support brace. This arch support will provide cushioning and make you feel comfortable. In addition, I'll give you an anti-inflammatory roll-on that you'll use three times a day. I'm also prescribing an anti-inflammatory medication that you'll take twice a day with food, which is for the inflammation. To help you stretch out the ligament, you'll have a stretching splint, and I'll see you next week to talk about making a customized orthotic— sometimes called an insert—that will take care of this problem long term."

Tell her that she'll experience relief from the pain but that you haven't eliminated the cause of the pain. "Mrs. Jones, it's important to keep your appointment, so we can eliminate the problem once and for all and get you back to running right away. We don't want the pain to get worse." Ask again if she has any questions, then tell her that the medical assistant will be in to tape her foot and go over the instructions again. The medical assistant usually has stretching exercises, but if the patient's in a lot of pain, I wait until the second week to start these exercises. Otherwise the stretching could be even more painful.

In my office, either the doctor or the medical assistant makes the follow-up appointment in the treatment room, which prevents a bottleneck at the front desk. Further, the patient has a hard time saying no to the doctor and there's not so much chitchat. For some reason, patients tend to show pictures of their dogs or grandchildren when they make an appointment at the front desk but not in the exam room.

When you make the appointment, be sure to mention the time of the appointment three times. Say something like: "Okay, how is next Tuesday, the thirtieth, at 10 a.m.? Great, then I'll see you next Tuesday at 10 a.m." As she checks out, the front staff also looks up the appointment and mentions it one more time. This is triple confirmation. Patients have a lot on their minds, and you've given them oodles of information, so be sure the appointment time registers in their brain.

Key Takeaways:

- Use the patient's name frequently throughout the conversation. Everyone likes the sound of their own name.

- Use only laymen terms.

- Use foot models and the drawing board during the presentation. Some patients learn through visual aids.

- Don't discuss the cost of the orthotics until the next visit. If they happen to ask you, answer like this: "Let's see if this is something you need, and we'll check with your insurance company then." If you tell them the costs now, there's a chance they won't come back. They might speak to a friend or relative about orthotics and get some negative feedback.

- The point is to get them better, and there's no way they'll permanently get better after the first visit. So, make sure they come back. Tell them why they need to come back and what will happen at that visit—and what will happen if they don't come back.

- Always explain why you're doing what you're doing.

Second Heel Pain Visit:

Continue to develop your relationship with the patient to establish trust. Ask her how she's doing and to rate her pain level. Review her problem again and demonstrate the tendon pulling. Talk to her about how she felt while the tape was on for the first few days compared to when she removed it. Usually the tape helps, so explain what it did to help. Now tell her that orthotics are a customized device that will keep her feet in the proper position, which will stop the tendon from pulling, just like the tape did.

Be careful not to jump in and start talking about the costs. In most cases, the problem with selling orthotics isn't the cost, it's your confidence in the product and how you present it. Patients have to feel comfortable that they're doing the right thing. If you hem and haw, if you have a lot of ums in your presentation, if you don't look the patient in the eye, and if you don't smile, it will be clear that you lack confidence.

Review the progress that's already been achieved. That means you need to take her back to last week when her pain was a 7 or 8. You must tell her what will happen if she doesn't get the orthotics! You can say something like this: "Mrs. Jones, do you see how the orthotics will help you? When you get them, you'll be back to running right away (or whatever her hot button was on the first visit). We don't want you to continue having that pain because then you'll favor your other foot, thus putting more pressure on it—and then that foot can become painful. Also, if we don't correct the pain, you can get knee, hip, or lower back pain." Demonstrate how this is so by standing up, rotating your foot out and pointing to the direction of the knee and hip joints. "Most people don't need surgery for this condition, but for the ones who do, it's because they waited too long before the problem was properly treated.

"To make the device, you will stand on our 3D scanner (you can also print out a picture of a patient's foot in stance via this scanner to show them the pressure points on their feet when standing and how this can be corrected) and we make corrections via the computer so that your feet will remain in the proper position. Then we prescribe the right device for you. The insert goes in whatever shoes you're wearing when you're walking. What kind of shoes do you wear when you're on your feet a lot?" (I don't care if the patient wears high heels, as long as they don't cause pain and if they aren't walking in them a lot.)

"The orthotics are guaranteed to fit in your shoes and to be comfortable. I make a lot of these devices, and my patients are really happy. The major shell of the device will last at least two to three years. The cover won't last forever, but it should last a couple of years and it's inexpensive to replace."

Just for the record, in my office, we scan patients' feet and we also cast them. I cast all serious athletes and children.

"The cost is $500.00. I will only need half down today and the other half when you pick them up in a couple of weeks. Unfortunately, your insurance doesn't cover them, but we'll send the claim in with a letter of medical necessity and do whatever we can to get you reimbursed."

At this point, say *absolutely nothing*. No matter how long the patient is silent, keep looking at her and wait for a response. You might be thinking that she thinks it's too expensive, but she might be considering how she's going to pay for it: from which account, with a credit card or check, or if she can borrow the money.

When she agrees to the purchase, reaffirm that she made a good decision. People don't want to spend their money if they're not sure the product will help them. You might mention that she can make both payments with her credit card. This is usually all you have to do.

Typical Questions or Objections:
- Do I have to pay for it all now? "You can postdate your checks if you'd like. The first half can be postdated by two weeks, and when you pick the inserts up in two weeks, you can postdate that check by two weeks." If

paying by credit card: "We can charge your card half today and the other half when you pick up the orthotics in about two weeks."

- I have to speak with my spouse. "I understand. You can call him/her right now (then leave the treatment room while the patient uses their cell phone). If you'd like, I can speak to him/her and explain about the inserts if you think that would help. By the way, do you think your spouse would mind if it would help you?"

- I'd like to call my insurance company first. "I understand, Mrs. Jones. However, we've dealt with this company before and know that they don't cover it. On numerous occasions, we've called the insurance company to verify the benefits, and they told us it was covered. But when we got the claim back, it was denied. Then we had to tell the patient that they owed the money, and they were very upset, as they should be. Nobody likes that kind of surprise. I hope you understand. I understand your concerns, but I will keep my promise to you and get you better."

A lot of times we call the insurance company just prior to seeing the patient, and we tell the patient the name of the person we spoke with. And we always get a reference number for proof that we made the call.

Key Takeaways:
- Notice that I didn't say that I guarantee that *the orthotics* will get them out of their pain 100 percent. I guarantee their comfort and that I will get them out of their pain.

- Don't give in after their first objection. People don't usually tell you the real reason why they won't do something right away. You must show that you care. People don't care how much you know until you show them how much you care. Caring is about getting through all the barriers to give them the treatment they need. They'll thank you later.

- After the patient agrees, the MA should come in with a sheet of paper that says that the patient was informed that the orthotics might not be covered by insurance, and they'll be responsible for the $500 charge. Ask the patient to sign the form. The form should say that in the case the insurance company denies the orthotics for any reason, the patient is responsible. We do encourage the patient to call the insurance company themselves if they want to. That way, if the patient gets false information, they'll then be upset with the insurance company, not us. If we get the information and pass it on to them, they might think we did it wrong or that we lied to them. You can find a copy of this form at www.drpeterwishnie.com/resources.

Factors That Affect Your Sales

Check Your Appearance: I usually wear a dress shirt, tie, and dress pants. You don't have to dress that way, but I'm not at my best when I dress too casually. Casual dress, casual attitude. This is true for me, but not for everyone. For example, my associate loves to wear his scrubs. When he's comfortable, he's relaxed, which makes it easier for him to sell his services. And he does a great job. The point is that he's neat. He doesn't wear dirty sneakers or wrinkled scrubs. They're clean and ironed.

In his book, *No B.S. Sales Success in The New Economy*, Dan S. Kennedy says, "If the packaging of products has an impact on how people regard those products, then the packaging of people must have an impact on how others regard those people." You're a doctor. You don't have to be boring or stuffy. You should have fun and crack a joke or two, but make sure you do it in style.

Remember Your Purpose: When you know your purpose, your *why*, you'll be able to sell more. Your why, like with most doctors, should include helping people. If you only offer services that the patient's insurance will accept, but not ones that will do the job more quickly and effectively, then you're doing the patient an injustice. Time and time again, patients have come to my office after seeing several other doctors who didn't recommend a certain service—a service that's part of the normal guidelines for that diagnosis.

For example, let's say a patient has had heel pain for three or four years. He's seen several podiatrists before coming to me. I ask him about his prior treatments, and he says, "Oral medication, stretching, and physical therapy."

Some will have a night splint, and some won't. Some will have received an injection or two and some did not, and some have custom orthotics, and some don't. The common factor is that the patients who get these devices have insurance that covers them. Some will admit that custom orthotics were recommended, but they couldn't afford them.

We must always treat the patient, not the insurance.

Our job is to get the patient better. We must always treat the patient, not the insurance. Tell the patient what she needs and let her decide if she can or cannot afford it. If she can't, then go for plan B or C. But if plan A is the best plan, don't accept the first no. If you truly come from the goodness of your heart and explain how important it is for her to get the orthotics, then the patient might change her mind because she can see that you care and that you really believe the devices will help her.

Expect Results: I used to have an associate who would look at the patient's insurance information before going in the treatment room. I could hear him mumble, "Oh no! They won't be able to get the orthotics." This statement alone showed me that the doctor didn't believe in the value of the product and didn't believe the patient could afford it.

Consider yourself. Why do you buy anything? It's because the product solves a problem you have. You can't get rid of those tough stains in your clothes, so you buy Stain Be Gone. Or you buy something because of how it makes you feel, even if it harms you. Like Marlboro cigarettes. Remember the Marlboro Man? He was cool. He could get any woman he wanted, and some men wanted to be just like him.

You also buy from people you like and trust, and these people have high energy. High energy people believe in their products and themselves. Before going into the treatment room, check your energy level. Put on a big and genuine smile. Then expect the patient to say yes to your recommendations.

> Before going into the treatment room, check
> your energy level. Put on a big and genuine smile.
> Then expect the patient to say yes
> to your recommendations.

Offer Proof: Some patients need proof that your recommendations will work for them. I'll use the example of orthotics again because it's the biggest thing we sell. Ask some patients who love their orthotics to write a testimonial. Get written permission to use their story and print them up on one side of a sheet of paper, using good paper stock. On the other side of the page, have a write-up about what orthotics are and what they do.

Wear orthotics yourself and make a pair for each staff member. Your medical assistants could be selling them for you. The best testimonials are ones that mention the benefits of the orthotics. What can the person do now that he/she couldn't do before he/she wore orthotics? You can also use video testimonials that play in your welcome area or in the treatment room.

Give Them a Guarantee: Guarantees give the patient comfort. In their mind, it prevents them from making a bad decision. It's also something that almost no one else in the medical field offers. I don't guarantee that orthotics will eliminate their pain, but I do guarantee that the product will last at least two to three years and that they'll be comfortable. If not, I'll remake them. If the new orthotic is still uncomfortable, I refund their money.

Yes, there's been a patient or two who wanted their money back, but that loss doesn't compare to the greater sales we've enjoyed because we give our patients a guarantee. If you believe in your product, then stand behind it. I leave the patient with these thoughts:

- Our patients love their orthotics, and most won't leave home without them.

- I don't simply make the orthotics and dispense them. I also make sure they fit well.

- I'll see you periodically to adjust your orthotics if needed.

Buyer's Remorse

Have you ever had a patient who agreed to purchase orthotics, then went home and called back to cancel the order? This is buyer's remorse. It happens a lot when people purchase big items, like cars, homes, an expensive dress or suit—and even orthotics.

Why does this happen? People buy on emotion and impulse. They love how they feel in that dress or in the car. They picture themselves driving down the highway with the top down on their convertible and the wind blowing their hair. The sun is out, and they feel simply amazing. Until they get home and their wife says, "What are you doing? We can't afford that!" Then the husband reluctantly calls the car dealer to cancel the order.

With orthotics, the patient goes home and their spouse says, "Oh, Aunt Sally had a pair of those. She hated them and threw them in the garbage." Then he or she calls your office and says they changed their mind.

You can prevent this by reminding your patients why they purchased the product. After a purchase, I tell them they made a great decision: "You're going to feel so much better, and you'll be running in no time." It's important to reiterate the value of the product to prevent order cancellations.

How to Handle Returns

What a crazy topic when it comes to medicine. Returns? Yes, because this is podiatry and patients get night splints and cam boots and all kinds of supplies. We've all had the patient who paid for the night splint and then wants to return it. Sometimes they return it in one week, and sometimes it's two months later. They swear they never used it, or they tell you that their friend had one that they used instead, or they found one cheaper online. Many of my coaching clients get so frustrated when this happens.

Let me tell you docs, you'll never get rich from selling night splints, so if a patient wants to return it, revert to Nordstrom's policy. Return anything any time. The goal is to make the patient happy. Don't disagree or argue with them. It will save you a patient and even possible referrals, and most of all, it will save you the aggravation. It also makes the front desk job a lot easier, and the staff will thank you for that.

Nordstrom started in Northern California. It was just a shoe store when it first opened, located where a tire store used to be. One day, a woman came to the store to return a tire. Most business owners would say, "Sorry, ma'am, we can't help you." But not Nordstrom. They took the tire and gave her a refund. No questions asked. Think about it: How much did Nordstrom lose? I think they saw an opportunity and ran with it. They now have a customer for life, and even if the woman never shopped at Nordstrom, they only lost a few dollars.

Your DME doesn't cost you that much, so don't sweat it. Maybe you win over a patient, and maybe you don't. You actually do it for your own sanity, plus you're bringing extra value for the patient. Be Nordstrom.

Selling can be easy or it can be hard. It boils down to belief in yourself, belief in your product, and belief in the patient and the results you deliver.

CHAPTER 10:

WOW! Them

"In this volatile business of ours, we can ill afford to rest on our laurels, even to pause in retrospect. Times and conditions change so rapidly that we must keep our aim constantly focused on the future." – Walt Disney

There are all kinds of customer service. There is *poor* customer service, which can be defined by rude or unfriendly staff. Poor service can also mean ignoring a patron, slow service, or anything considered below par. Then there is *fair* service. You ask for chicken noodle soup and you get chicken noodle soup. You don't have to wait too long and the price is reasonable. Nothing special. The server is pleasant but not really excited to be there. After fair service comes *good* service. That's when you get what you ask for, the food is good but not amazing, the server is pleasant and even smiles, and the food comes out in a timely manner. Good service is not great service, and without great service, you cannot *WOW!* anybody.

If you want an abundant number of referrals, then you must provide *WOW!* customer service—service that goes above and beyond and gives your patient something to talk about.

If you want an abundant number of referrals, then you must provide *WOW!* customer service—service that goes above and beyond and gives your patient something to talk about.

If you provide poor service, the patient will tell ten people how bad you are. If you provide okay service or service that's just satisfying, the patient won't talk about you at all. If your service is merely good, they might mention you to one or two people. But if you provide *WOW!* customer service, your patient will write great reviews about you, talk about you in a Facebook group, and personally recommend you to five to ten people.

On top of that, providing *WOW!* customer service is the cheapest form of marketing you can find. Advertising your services to get new patients through your door can be very expensive, but once you get a new patient, you can make that patient's experience a phenomenal one. Now this patient becomes a referral machine.

Train a *WOW!* Staff

Is providing *WOW!* customer service costly? Sometimes doctors think that in order to provide an extraordinary patient experience, he or she must pay for a lot of extra goodies, like fresh baked cookies, coffee and water, snacks, an office brochure, massage chairs, etc. All these perks are nice, and I do recommend you do some or all of these things. But if you ask your patients what they want, they'll tell you they want to be seen on time, they don't want any surprise costs, and they want you to fully explain the treatment to them in non-medical terms.

The least expensive way to provide *WOW!* service is to be sure your staff is fully trained and can answer the patients' questions. Your staff must be competent. They need to either know the answers to patients' questions or to get the answer immediately. This is why training and re-training your staff is so important.

The staff must be extremely friendly and go out of their way to help the patients. Again, a warm, friendly smile goes a long way. I can tell you that most offices don't offer a warm, personal greeting. It's sad, but people no longer expect someone else to be nice to them. So, being nice and going out of your way is a differentiator for providing *WOW!* service.

Each individual person on your staff might be great at their job, but the complete team cannot be less than efficient—which can happen if you're shorthanded or the staff doesn't work well together. Most businesses over-work their staff. Bosses expect them to multi-task and get a lot accomplished in one day. But would you rather have your staff do multiple tasks half-assed, or do just a few things amazingly? Bosses don't like to hire people, and they especially despise training them. That's why the exemplary staff members are asked to perform so many tasks; they're simply reliable. But it rarely works out in the long run.

Business owners hate to spend money, and hiring more people means additional expense. But if you look at the return on investment that an additional person could bring, you can look at the expense from a different point of view. If the new hire is paid between $15 and $20 per per hour, and you're able to provide better service and have less errors because of them—which ultimately translates into more referrals and increased revenue—wouldn't it be worth it?

WOW! service begins with how you value and take care of your staff.

WOW! service begins with how you value and take care of your staff. If you treat them like you treat your patients, then they'll treat your patients just like they are treated.

Disney calls their customers "guests" and their staff "cast members." If you want to really learn how to treat the people around you, then I suggest you study the ins and outs of Disney. Have you ever heard people say they had a terrible experience at Disney World or Disneyland? Of course not! What Disney does is simply amazing. Think about it. Everyone knows how expensive it is to go there, and people do complain about that, but they ultimately say it's worth every penny just to see the smile on their child's or grandchild's face. Wouldn't it be great if every patient was that happy to pay you? I'm not sure that doctors can ever get to that point, but you definitely can try.

You'll never, ever make everyone happy. We have a harder job than Disney because our patients come in with pain. No one's excited about seeing us. They dread coming in because of the big three: time, fear, and money. We have a long way to go to make a patient happy. It's a challenge, but it's well worth the effort when you see your patient smiling and they're grateful for your service—just like grandma when she sees her little one smiling and licking that big rainbow lollipop.

Walt Disney said, "You don't build it for yourself. You know what people want, and you build it for them." What a true statement! Whatever you do in life, do it for others. I promise that you'll receive back ten times what you give out.

I've learned a lot from Disney. Years ago, I took my whole staff to a Disney Institute seminar on customer service for the health industry. I spent a lot of money that day, but it was well worth it. My staff totally understood the message I wanted to convey. Sometimes you need to take your staff out of the office for them to learn on their own and to be part of something bigger. It also allows them to mingle with other staff from different offices. They then come back with some great ideas.

But, doctor, you must go with them! It's terribly disappointing for them to come back really excited about sharing some great ideas from the seminar if you don't implement them. Sometimes the ideas require an outlay of money, and if you weren't there, you won't understand why you should pay for this new thing. Just like when a patient goes home and tells their spouse they want to spend $500 on a pair of orthotics. The spouse wasn't at the appointment and doesn't understand what orthotics are or what they do, so they say, "We can't afford it." (By the way, when this happens, try to get the spouse on the phone right there in the office. I've sold many pairs of orthotics this way.)

Details, Details, Details

WOW! service means that you pay attention to every little detail. Make sure your office is modern and clean. Go in your bathrooms. Do they look clean and smell nice? This is critically important. When looking for a new home, people—especially women—look at the kitchen and bathrooms first. To a patient, a dirty bathroom is a sign of dirty instruments.

If you don't pay attention to details, it shows that you don't care. If you see a piece of paper on the floor, pick it up. Don't leave it for your staff. Your staff will follow your lead. Lead by example. If you've trained your staff properly and they've bought into the company's culture and vision, they'll make sure the office is clean and presentable.

WOW! service means keeping your promises and having speedy delivery. If you or your staff promises something to a patient, make sure you deliver. If you tell them their orthotics will be ready in two weeks, they must be available for pickup in two weeks. If they don't arrive on time, apologize to the patient, but also call the lab to see if you can put in a rush order. You might have to pay extra for that, but the goal is to keep the patient happy. You'll still make a profit on the devices.

We developed a system in our office to make sure the patients' orders arrive on time, called the Order Status System. It's very easy and simple because everything is tracked on an Excel spreadsheet that we keep on our server, so everyone can access it—even our satellite office. Whenever we order a pair of shoes, braces, or orthotics for the patient, the medical assistants add the order to the Excel sheet. Across the top, the columns have the patient's name, the order date, what was ordered, and if it has arrived. When the device arrives, the front desk enters that date on the sheet.

We check the order status at least twice a week. If an undelivered order is approaching the two-week deadline, we call the company to check its status. If it's delayed, we call the patient to tell him or her, and we let them know that we'll keep them posted. Even better, we get a specific arrival date from the company, add a couple of days to the so-called promise date and tell the patient it will arrive by then. You'll look like a hero if the product arrives sooner. Always under-promise and over-deliver. That's *WOW!* customer service.

Remember the Purpose

By now, you've built a great staff that has empathy for your patients and is also very courteous. They treat people the way they want to be treated and have respect for the elderly and children, as well as all different cultures, races, and sexual orientations. They must each know their own role and purpose and understand and embrace the organization's purpose.

For example, think about the person who cuts your hair—I'm speaking to the men here. I don't go to a barber; I go to a hairstylist. She cuts and styles whatever hair I have left, but she also trims my eyebrows. Sometimes she'll forget the eyebrows and I have to remind her. I once told her, "If you considered yourself a head groomer, then you'd take care of everything on my face and scalp." Of course, head groomer sounds like the person who cuts your dog's hair, so it's not really a good description. The point is that if she understood her purpose, she wouldn't forget any part of her job.

Another example is a police officer. Their purpose is to keep the public safe while making sure the citizens obey the laws. In Texas, they're very nice. I remember going to a Texas Rangers baseball game and I, along with many fans, was crossing the street to get to the stadium. The police officers wore their cowboy police hats and were so polite to all the people. They said things like, "This way, ma'am," and, "Enjoy the game, sir."

Now compare that to my hometown, New York City. At our baseball games, they usually say things like, "Keep it moving," or, "Let's go." And if you ask an NYC cop for directions, they just point and grunt. Now, to stand up for the fine men in blue in NYC, I have to say that they have a really tough job. We have a lot more people and moving parts in New York, and the police are trying to observe everything around them. But imagine if they agreed that their purpose was to provide safety to the public and make sure the citizens obey the laws while being courteous and showing respect for everyone. In return, they would probably get the respect they so deserve.

Keeping Score

Think about your patient care coordinator at the front desk. His or her purpose is to fill the appointment book with productive patients, make sure the patients keep their appointments, and collect all monies due at the time of service, as well as past balances. When you combine those responsibilities with embracing the organization's purpose to have raving patients who are 100 percent happy, who are educated in their foot and ankle problems, who refer others, and who pay their bills on time, the PCC will know exactly *what* to do.

The *how* part comes with exceptional training. Goals are important in providing *WOW!* service because reaching them causes the practice to thrive, and people like to work in a thriving environment. Making patients happy is one of our goals, and if you want to know if they're happy, you have to keep score. Happy patients come back for their appointments and refer others, and you can know this by looking at your numbers.

Take the example of a 3-on-3 pickup basketball game—only three people on each team. No one's really keeping score. It's just a group of people having fun. Do you know what that game looks like? It's chaotic. There's usually a ball hog that always takes the shot. Defense is nonexistent, and there are a lot of turnovers.

Now, take that same game, but this time keep score. The first team to reach ten points gets a bonus of $100 per player. What does that game look like? The defense definitely shows up, and there will be a lot more passing to the open teammate. When you keep score, you know how many more points you need to win. Knowing your numbers allows you to change direction and change the pace of the game.

You can also know if your patients are happy by looking at your reviews and by asking your patients to participate in a survey. You can do this by sending them an online questionnaire. Go to www.drpeterwishnie.com/resources for a survey we've used.

Efficiency comes with practice. Just like the saying goes, practice makes perfect. *WOW!* customer service starts when your team members perform their jobs without even thinking about it. That's why training, re-training, goal setting, and keeping score is so vital to *WOW!*ing your patients.

Providing *WOW!* service means you understand your patients and have the ability to deliver their desired services and results. Be sure you understand what the patient really wants; don't assume you know what it is. During the interview process, ask her to define the desired outcome. It might not be to fix the bunion through surgery. She just might want a quick "fix" for now—an injection or an orthotic—because her vacation is coming up. Of course, you need to explain to her what could possibly happen in the next few years if the bunion gets worse, but the patient still has the right to decide for herself. That's why you make all the options available to your patients.

The Disney Institute wrote a book with Theodore Kinni titled *Be Our Guest: Perfecting the Art of Customer Service.* In this book, they described the four elements of quality standards. The credit for these elements goes to Dick Nunis, who became chairman of Walt Disney Attractions. These four elements—in order—are safety, courtesy, show, and efficiency. If it's good for Disney, it's good for podiatry. Here's how to use all four elements in your practice.

Safety: You must ensure safety, not just for your patients, but for your staff, as well. In terms of syringe safety, the location of your sharps containers is important. After you finish giving an injection, don't put the syringe and needle back in the debris tray that's attached to your chair. Immediately dispose of it in your sharps container. Don't leave any sharps in this tray. Take off the blades for your assistant. Make sure your assistants clean all the trays and floors between patients. Don't leave any bloody gauze around. The outlets around the office should have safety plugs, so young children don't put their fingers in them. Children's toys should be clean and safe. There should be handrails in your X-ray room and in the bathrooms for the elderly and others.

Courtesy: Treat people the way they want to be treated. I tell my staff to "treat the patients like they're your grandmother." Not everyone loves their mother, but almost everyone loves their grandmother. Open doors for the patients, and don't walk too far ahead of them when escorting them into the treatment rooms. Call them by the name they prefer. If they say, "My name is Mrs. Jones," don't call them by their first name. I say my name is Peter, but some people call me Pete—and the only time I like to be called Pete is on the baseball field or in the gym because it sounds kind of tough in those arenas. Otherwise I despise being called Pete. Be sensitive to your patients' preferences.

Here are some *WOW!* tips regarding courtesy. Call all your new patients the day after their appointment to see if they have any additional questions. Sometimes they'll remember a question they wanted to ask you but forgot until they got home. I once had a new associate who was resistant to calling the patients because he thought the patient might feel he wasn't confident in the treatment plan. I told the young doctor that the call wasn't to check if the patient is feeling better. It's to ask them if they have any additional questions. Then you can ask how they're feeling. This demonstrates empathy and that you simply care, which means that they'll be more likely to keep their next appointment.

It's best for you, the doctor, to make these calls, not the staff. There's a bigger *WOW!* effect when you make the call; the patients simply can't believe you took the time to do this. They'll tell all their friends about it the next time they go out to dinner. If you think you can't find the time to do this, here's a little trick. Have one of your staff e-mail you the patients' phone numbers, and during your drive home, just click the number and you can speak to the patient hands-free. All your calls will be done by the time you get home. Most of the patients won't be available, so all you have to do is leave a message.

Another courteous *WOW!* thing I do is to check on my patients for non-podiatric related situations. If a patient is nervous because she's going for a breast biopsy to rule out cancer, I call her a few days after the biopsy to check on her. Think of your patients as family, not just a foot and ankle problem to solve.

Show: Doctor, the show begins with you. The moment you step in the office, the show begins. You set the tone of the office for the day. If you're sulking, the staff will too. If you expect your staff to come in all shiny with high energy every day, then you need to do that.

Of course, you're human and you'll hit some bumps—sometimes giant mounds—in the road that can affect your day. Just recognize this *before* you enter the office. I sometimes sit in my car and put on the Bruce Springsteen song "Born to Run," and get psyched up before going into the office. All great performers and athletes do this.

We are truly entertainers. We are putting on a show, and this show has a very long run, longer than *Phantom of the Opera*! Do whatever it takes to get yourself in the right mood, which is where self-talk comes in. I have affirmation cards that I read to myself every morning.

- I love my patients and they love me.

- Things come easy to me.

- I can handle anything that comes my way.

- I listen to my staff and patients with intent.

- I don't get defensive and jump to conclusions too quickly. I ask questions and listen.

- People are interested in my opinion.

I also review my goals every morning, which includes my purpose. Now here's the key to overcoming obstacles in your life—drum roll please! *Be grateful.* Write down three to five things you're grateful for every morning or every evening. Be specific. What did little Johnnie or Jennie do that makes you feel grateful? Don't be grateful for only the big things. Be grateful the sun came out, the grass is green, and the flowers are blooming. What about that cup of coffee you're having? Be grateful for the UPS man who brings in your medical supplies, so you can help your patients.

Gratitude is everything. We love to focus on what we don't have, but you have a lot to be grateful for. In our society, it's easy to compare yourself to others, thanks to social media. Everyone on Instagram looks fabulous and leads such a wonderful life. Phooey. Every successful person has either had or is having some issues. It's called life. You cannot appreciate your successes without the failures. It might sound crazy, but be grateful for these failures, because a failure is something that was meant to be.

Picture that the door handle on the treatment room has a bolt of lightning going through it. As soon as you touch this handle, a wave of energy starts to run through your body. Before opening the door, this bolt of energy has perked you up, and you now have a big smile on your face. That's how you enter the treatment room—every time.

A word of caution. Don't be overly enthusiastic, because you don't yet know what's on the other side of the door. The patient could be in a cranky mood and can become even more upset if he or she sees an overly sunshiny appearance. Just wear a nice smile and immediately look at your patient to read his or her mood. Shake their hand and get a feel for their disposition. If they aren't smiling back and seem a little grumpy, then ask them about it. Ask how you can help. If it's foot related, show them you understand their frustration and that you'll do whatever it takes to get them better. Empathy goes a long way.

Efficiency: You absolutely must be on time, every time. Then make sure your staff is on time, too. The great football coach Vince Lombardi said, "If you're five minutes early, then you're ten minutes late." Make sure you arrive fifteen to thirty minutes prior to the start of the day. Get your coffee, open the computer, and get your day going. Go over the morning schedule with your staff. Have everything ready prior to the patient's appointment. Get all the orthotics that will be dispensed for the day pulled. Have all blood test results and MRI reports printed prior to the appointment. Even though the reports are in our EMR, I like to print them, so I can give the patient a copy. That also makes it easier to review the report with them.

Check out the lists I've made of some ways you can *WOW!* your patients during all phases of their experience with you and your office. Some ideas are over the top and will inspire you to think of ways you can incorporate them. For example, if you don't have efficient parking at your office, you can offer valet service. A little bit over the top—and unusual—but imagine what your patients would think if you implemented this idea. I'm sure you'd be the talk of the town. Further, if you ever want to stop accepting insurances, then you'll need to provide these Tiffany-style services to get your patients to pay. You won't have as many patients as you do now, but you won't need to because your overhead will decrease, and your patients will be paying you cash.

Before the Appointment
- Send the patient a welcome packet that includes:
    - Welcome letter
    - Staff and doctor bios
    - Practice brochure
    - Diagnosis brochure
    - Personalized directions with map
    - Magnet
    - Business cards
    - All forms to fill out prior to their appointment
- Verify the patient's benefits

The *WOW!* Arrival
- Offer valet parking
- Give a friendly greeting
- A presentable welcome area (waiting room)
- Play pleasant music
- Make sure the office has a pleasant aroma
- Be sure your staff is professionally dressed
- Have coffee available
- Display fresh flowers

The Check-In
- Thank them for completing the paperwork before their arrival
- Offer them a warm, fresh cookie
- Give them a big, friendly smile

The Not-So-Long Wait
- Have massage chairs
- Offer snacks and drinks
- Deliver warm wash cloths on a silver tray using tongs
- Have a loop of testimonials playing on video; display letters and photos of happy patients in a book; show pictures of celebrities with the doctor

Staff Phone Calls
- Smile and be friendly while speaking on the phone
- Have a welcoming salutation
- Be courteous
- Use patient's name at least three times
- End the call with, "Remember, my name is Roxy, and if you need anything when you get here, just let me know."

Physical Changes to the Office
- Make design changes to update your office
- Have beautiful pictures in the hallways
- Have posters, music, color, and fragrant aroma in treatment rooms
- Play educational videos in treatment rooms
- Make sure the lighting is bright, not dull

Checking Out
This is the best time to *WOW!* your patients even more, so they will refer you to others.
- Say, "How was your visit?"
- Provide a patient education kit
- Provide before and after surgery pictures
- Ask, "Who do you know who has a foot or ankle problem?"

Post-Appointment
- Send a thank-you letter
- Send a gift to the person who referred that patient
- Physician phone call the next day
- Send a pastry or video and popcorn to post-op patients
- Call patients regarding non-related podiatry tests
- Create a system to remember patients' hobbies

Service
- Give pizza gift certificates to surgical patients
- Small acts of kindness: changing their tire in an emergency, walk patients out with an umbrella if it's raining, deliver shoes/orthotics to patient's homes when they can't come to the office

- Set up a referral program
- Thank them with a spa gift card
- Give out Dunkin' Donuts gift cards
- Put a lottery ticket in their birthday card
- Tell them about seasonal specials and promotions
- Give patients treatment folders explaining their condition and treatment options
- Send them quality control surveys
- Give them a referral packet
- Give out free books, including a children's coloring book (visit Top-practices.com to get more information on all books)

There's only one way to guarantee to fill your treatment rooms on a daily basis and that's by providing consistent *WOW!* service. And if you implement some—or all—of the ideas in this chapter, your patients will come back and bring others with them.

CHAPTER 11:

Money Makes the World Go Around

"Money often costs too much." – Ralph Waldo Emerson

How ironic. I didn't do this on purpose, but we are discussing your finances in chapter 11. And this chapter is about *how not to file chapter 11!*

You work hard to make your money, but it shouldn't be hard or expensive to collect it. The bottom line is that you can't help people if you don't have a thriving business. Most doctors have a hard time separating the business side from the patient care side. So, you may try to avoid talking to your patients about money because you're concerned that you'll come across as a money-hungry doctor. But these conversations can't be avoided. If you're not comfortable discussing money, delegate it to someone else.

> You work hard to make your money, but it shouldn't be hard or expensive to collect it.

It's interesting that patients often come in thinking they already know their diagnosis, but they have no idea that they have a deductible or a co-pay. It's up to us to educate them.

Patients have the right to know the costs before any treatment is rendered. However, this isn't always possible in medicine. Because patients want and expect to know the costs prior to treatment, you need to get their insurance information before they come in for their appointment. In my office, we ask for this information over the phone, then have one of our college students call the insurance company to find out about the patient's benefits. In addition to deductibles and co-payments, we get information about the patient's coverage on all DME, including orthotics. We also check to see if there's a limit on podiatry coverage and if the insurance will cover more than one pair of orthotics, just in case the patient needs a second pair.

The hard part is that we can't guarantee that the information we receive is accurate. How many times have you told a patient that their insurance covers an item, only to find out this wasn't true? It's very frustrating. We want to do what's best for our patients, and they get better faster when there's less confusion over financial matters. But even though you check with their insurance company about the allowed amounts for each code, there can still be inaccuracies, which can lead to unexpected bills and disgruntled patients. The solution is to have great communication with the patient. We put everything in writing to prevent any possible problems down the road.

Even when you have great communication with your patients, some of them will still be unhappy. No matter what you do or what you say, there will be patients who complain. I call these patients the one percenters. If you're lucky enough to have a very busy practice, the one percenters will add up. So, don't focus on those people. Instead, focus on the 99 percent who are reasonable. If you shift your focus, you'll love your practice, and your sanity will thank you.

Collections Conversations

Your rate of collections depends upon what, how, and when you talk to your patients. Those people whose accounts are only five to fifteen days late will be more responsive to your collection efforts. Not only will you collect more by calling these patients, you'll teach them not to become 45-, 60-, or 90-day late patients.

For example, Mrs. Jones's payment was due on the fifteenth. Today is the twentieth, and you still don't have her payment. In this case, you'll make a call that's a friendly "what happened?" call.

You could say something like this: "Mrs. Jones, this is Mary from Dr. Baker's office. I haven't received your payment yet. Did it get hung up in the mail?" Have the ability to take credit cards or even a check over the phone in case she's prepared to pay right now. Write down the result of the conversation in the patient's EMR. If she doesn't pay over the phone, get a commitment for a payment date, and if you don't get her payment on that day, call her back immediately. Don't wait to send out a statement.

Some patients will ask about making payment arrangements, and my best answer is *don't do it*. At times, you may have to make special arrangements, but you want to avoid this as much as possible. The problem with payment arrangements is that patients usually don't honor them. And when they don't, it costs you money to send a statement or make a phone call, and that decreases your profit margin considerably.

So, how do you get around it? When the patient is in the office, tell him the cost of the service that may not be covered by his insurance. Even if it is covered, he might have a high deductible that he hasn't yet met. If he asks if you accept payments, the right answer is, "I'm sorry, but we don't." In most cases, patients are fine with that. They just wanted to know if you'd make an arrangement. Tell him he can pay with a credit card, cash, check, or even a medical credit card like CareCredit.

Early in my practice, I took postdated checks, but today most people don't carry a checkbook. One time, I made a payment arrangement with a patient who owed me $1,200 for surgery. She agreed to pay $100 a month for twelve months and wrote out twelve postdated checks. As a courtesy, we called her each month prior to depositing one of them.

Reports

Look at your total accounts receivable every month. Remember:

- Total A/R should be no more than two months gross billing.

- The 0-30 days category should be higher than the others because you just did the work and are waiting for payment.

- The 61-90 days outstanding A/R should be less than your 31-60 days A/R.

- Anything ninety days past due or over should be less than 15 percent of your total A/R. Anything over ninety days is difficult to collect.

- The 121-180 days bucket may higher than the others because you've left uncollectable funds in your account. Clean up these accounts and write off anything you can't collect.

Next, run an aging report by insurance company. In other words, list all of the Blue Cross open accounts with patient names and information. Start off with the 61-90 days bucket and call the insurance company that owes you the most. Go through each account and find out the reasons for non-payment. If the answer you get is unsatisfactory, then ask for that person's supervisor. Get promises for payment and document the results of each call. Ask for a reference number and the name of the representative on that call.

Educate Your Patients

Almost every problem you'll ever encounter regarding money will be because of faulty communication with your patient prior to the treatment. Patient education is critically important.

You must have key people onsite to discuss finances with your patients, whether you have an outside biller or not. Train at least two people to discuss insurance benefits and costs with your patients. If your practice is large enough, you can have a dedicated person whose sole purpose is to be the financial liaison, but you still need a second person who's trained in insurance education to fill in when needed.

How to be Prepared

- Become familiar with all types of insurance that your office accepts. Maintain an insurance binder with photographs of all the types of insurance cards your patients present. On each page, write whether or not your office participates with that plan. Circle key numbers that are on the card and write down their meaning on the sheet. Circle the amount of the specialist co-pay versus the co-pay for a primary care physician. This binder will be a continuing source of training for every single employee.

    Remember that your assistants dispense products that may or may not be covered by insurance, so everyone in your office needs to be educated on insurance matters.

- Study all the insurance plans yourself, so you can explain the plan parameters to your patients with confidence.

- Know the difference between in-network and out-of-network providers and the benefits the patient can access in your office.

- Be able to sell your patients on the type of care they'll receive by choosing your office.

- Know how to explain the difference between covered and non-covered benefits and how they're affected by the patient's deductible. Patients can be confused when they get a bill for a service that you said is covered. It might be covered, but they may not have met their deductible and have to pay out of pocket.

- Assure your patients that your office will do everything to work with their plan to get the maximum benefit available from their insurance company.

- Demonstrate how your office makes it easy for your patients to benefit from their insurance plan. Tell them that you file all their claims and will follow up with the insurance company to get the reimbursement as quickly as possible.

When your patient understands that their insurance plan isn't their treatment plan, communicating about the costs becomes relatively easy.

: : : :

Phone Scenarios: How to Ask for Money Up Front and Handle All Objections

Here are some typical questions and objections you may hear from patients as they begin to get a better understanding of their insurance plan and benefits. Helpful responses are suggested.

What? My insurance company won't pay for it?

Being empathetic, not sympathetic, means showing that you understand their concern. You can say, "I understand your concern," or, "I'm glad you mentioned it so I can help you." Educate your patients about insurance limitations—with *every* new patient that walks through your door. If you educate them in the beginning, it won't come back to bite you when you deliver your treatment plan.

Your fees are too high!

Never get defensive or feel like you're being attacked. If a patient expresses this objection, it means they don't see the value in your service. People will pay for value. So, go back and review your interactions with this patient. Did you spend quality time with them? Did you answer all their questions? Did you fully explain their foot problem and go over all the types of treatment? If you did all these things, it's unlikely that they will make this complaint.

But if they do, here are the steps to take. Some patients think you get paid what you charge, but tell them that you only receive what the insurance company allows. Emphasize that your rates don't cause their insurance premiums to increase. Stand 100 percent behind your work and be committed to ensure their complete satisfaction. Make sure the staff demonstrates that your office intends to exceed their expectations.

In a nutshell, if you provide value and educate the patient about their financial obligations as well as their foot problem, you'll rarely hear this complaint.

In a nutshell, if you provide value and educate the patient about their financial obligations as well as their foot problem, you'll rarely hear this complaint.

I only want what my insurance covers.

You can handle this objection by educating your patient about their insurance benefits. If he mentions this, it's because he is worried about costs. He might think that many of your services aren't covered. If his insurance covers your services, then there's no issue, but if you want to prescribe a night splint or any other form of DME and it isn't covered—or it's covered and he has a separate deductible for DME—then you need to explain why he needs this service and how it will help him. Never discuss cost before the patient agrees that he needs the treatment.

What? Laser treatments aren't covered by my insurance?

Of course, you'll be selling some treatments that aren't covered by any insurance plan. Selling was covered in detail in chapter 9, but let's go over this potential scenario. Note that this approach will only work if you've already developed a rapport with the patient and gained their trust.

Staff: "The fee today for your laser treatment is $1,000 today." (Note: I mention the word today twice because patients often ask, "Do I have to pay for that today?").

Patient: "What about my insurance? They should pay part of this cost."

Staff: "Mr. Brown, that's a very good question. The procedure is considered cosmetic, and your plan does not cover this treatment."

Patient: "That's unbelievable! I pay so much money for this plan, and now it doesn't pay for what I need."

Staff: "I know exactly how you feel. I understand your disappointment, and I know that this treatment is important to you. I also know that you don't like to be in pain (you can substitute a phrase about ugly nails if the laser treatment was for fungus)."

Patient: "Okay."

The reason you sell treatment not covered by insurance is to help your patients receive the treatment they need and want without regard to insurance limitations and barriers. Don't beat around the bush. Be straight with your patients and tell them up front about the costs so they're not surprised when you ask for payment.

I don't want to pay until the treatment is complete.

A patient may say this because they want to buy some time or they think that if they're not satisfied, they won't have to pay. But this isn't an option.

Since most of our treatments are started and finished on the same day, you might only hear this request in regard to laser treatments or prior to surgery. Sometimes the patient asks for payment plans for the laser treatment, and we simply say that we can't do that. Reassure the patient that many of your other patients have gotten great results with the laser and that you're confident they will, too.

If they're having surgery, we ask the patient to pay the minimum amount they will owe according to their insurance *before* their surgery. At this point, we've already called their insurance company and were told the allowable amount for the procedure. We tell the patient that we collect that minimum because insurance companies sometimes give us the wrong information. Then we ask the patient to sign a form that fully explains this information, which usually isn't a problem.

Your staff should be fully trained to answer these types of questions without getting flustered, confused, or thrown for a loop.

Your staff should be fully trained to answer these types of questions without getting flustered, confused, or thrown for a loop. Make sure they are 100 percent confident in what they will say, and role play with them to make sure that they are. Emphasize that they should never use the phrase "office policy" when answering a patient's question or concern. Instead, they should explain the reasons behind the policy in terms of the benefits to the patient.

Sometimes You Just Need a Three-Way!

I know this has happened to you before: a patient questions your staff member's competency and claims he didn't get the right information from the insurance company. Or the patient was supposed to provide information to their insurance company, but failed to do so. These are great times to make a three-way call between your staff, the patient, and the insurance company. Your patient will pay you faster when they hear the information directly from the insurance representative.

Past-Due Accounts

What happens when an invoice reaches ninety days past due? That's when we send the patient a final notice that is big, bold, and scary. It's the statement prior to sending the account to collections. If we still don't receive payment, we call the patient one more time, one to two weeks after the notice was sent. If there's no response, we send the patient to collections and remove this balance from the A/R.

In most cases, you'll only see this money when the patient applies for a mortgage or needs to buy a car. Otherwise, kiss that money goodbye. All you can do is learn from this experience. Did you follow your procedures prior to treating the patient, as well as during the patient's visits? If so, then it's just the cost of doing business, no need to fret about it. Go to www.drpeterwishnie.com/resources for samples of collection letters and notices.

When you send someone to collections, certain patients may threaten you. They'll say things like, "I'm not paying because I'm still in pain," or "I'm going to sue you for malpractice." In most cases, these are harmless threats and a way for them to try to scare you so you'll erase their balance. Don't fall for it.

I've instructed my financial department to let me know before they send any patient to collections. As the doctor, I know my patients best. If the surgical patient is still being treated post-operatively, then I'll hold off on the collection matter. I want to get them mobile again, and I don't want finances to get in the way of their treatment. That being said, it's rare that my surgical patients have any issues with my office during their post-operative care because we explain the finances prior to surgery and we collect all monies up front. Although there could still be a balance due, it's usually small and collectable.

You can be the best darned doctor in the world, but you can't help anyone unless you run a profitable business. If you go out of business, how can you help your patients? Even though your business is to help others, you're actually in the business of running a business. The best way to be profitable is to collect every dollar that is owed to you.

How to Get Paid Quickly

The flow chart on page 136 is a visual depiction of how to get paid quickly. A few key points when dissecting this chart:

- During the patient's visit, enter the charges in the billing software. I frequently hear doctors say that they didn't enter their charges because the electronic medical notes weren't finished. What does one have to do with the other? If you can't get your notes finished, at least enter the diagnosis and procedures either in your notes or in your billing software. In my office, the doctor enters the codes. There's no superbill that has the potential to get lost. You want to make sure you get paid as quickly as possible. You have your own bills to pay and can't afford to wait for your money. When you enter all the charges at the time of service, your claims can be submitted the following day.

- The next step is to generate and print a report for all the claims submitted that day. This report is filed in what we call a *tickler*. Tickler files, for you non-baby boomers, are a collection of date-labeled file folders where time-sensitive documents are filed according to the future date when action must be taken. In our office, we have twelve tabs, one for each month. For each month we have thirty to thirty-one folders, one for each day of the month. You would put the claims reports in the folder representing three weeks from the date of service. The claims should be paid by that date, but if not, you can follow up on each one of them easily because the paperwork is in the file. Of course, you can also make folders on your computer and follow the same system. The point is to have a system that allows you to follow up on each claim.

- When you receive the explanation of benefits from the insurance company, you might discover that the patient now has a balance due. Send a statement to the patient immediately, then call them in ten days to follow up. You can take the payment over the phone or get a commitment from them to pay. If the patient gives you a promise date for payment, put in a reminder to call the patient three days later if you didn't get paid. Combining phone calls with paper statements is more effective than sending statements alone.

- Be aware of their next appointment date. If the balance is small and they're coming in within the next week, ask them to pay at that time, rather than phoning them. In that case, put a note in the patient's chart to remind the front desk to collect the balance when they come in. If the patient gives you a promise date for payment, put in a reminder to call the patient three days later if you didn't get paid.

- When a bill reaches ninety days past due, we send a big red statement with the words **STATEMENT OF DELINQUENCY** on top. This is their last notice before we send them to collections.

How to Make Sure You Collect All of Your Money

- Verify and know your patient's benefits prior to their arrival. You may need to hire another employee or have a current staff member do the job part-time. You can also hire a very smart high school or college student to the job. Create a form that the staff member reads to ask all the questions about the patient's benefits that you need to collect. Put that information into the patient's electronic chart.

- When the patient arrives, a member of the financial team will sit down with them to review their benefits. This can be done in a private room or even in the treatment room. The key is total privacy.

- The patient signs a financial form that states that he or she understands the financial information given to them.

- For the major procedures that you perform, create a fee schedule for your top insurance companies than can be quickly referenced.

Flow of a Bill

How a Bill Gets Paid

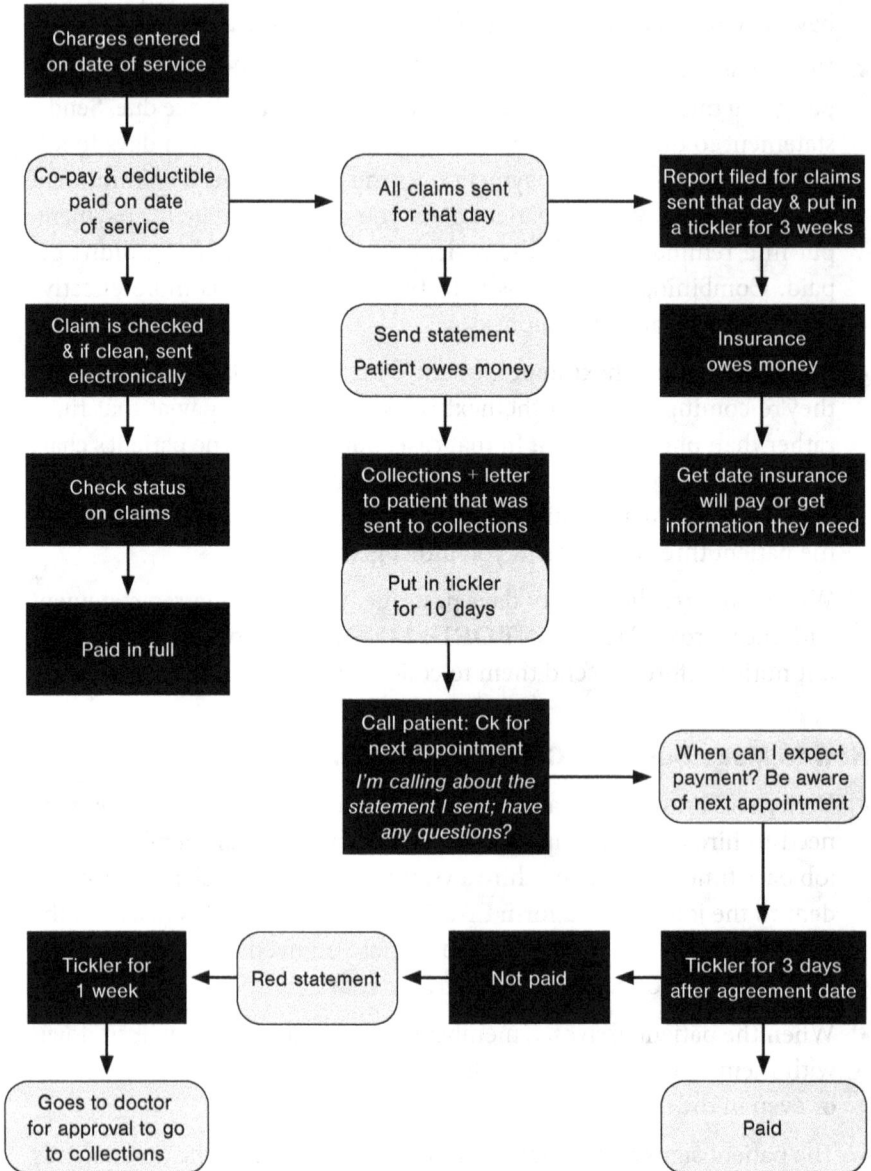

Charges entered on date of service

Co-pay & deductible paid on date of service

Claim is checked & if clean, sent electronically

Check status on claims

Paid in full

All claims sent for that day

Send statement Patient owes money

Collections + letter to patient that was sent to collections

Put in tickler for 10 days

Call patient: Ck for next appointment
I'm calling about the statement I sent; have any questions?

When can I expect payment? Be aware of next appointment

Report filed for claims sent that day & put in a tickler for 3 weeks

Insurance owes money

Get date insurance will pay or get information they need

Tickler for 1 week

Red statement

Not paid

Tickler for 3 days after agreement date

Goes to doctor for approval to go to collections

Paid

- Inform the patient every time you're about to perform a procedure that isn't covered by their insurance. When they agree to pay, ask them to sign a form of understanding and agreement of payment at the time of service. Be sure to say, "Mr. Jones, payment is due today." Otherwise they might think that they pay next time or on a payment plan. You need to use the word today when you talk about payment.

- Train your front staff to collect all monies due at the time of service, as well as any past balances the patient may be carrying. If the patient leaves your office without paying, your collection team will have to call, send statements, call again, and send a few more statements. This can cause the patient to resent and dislike you and your practice. Happy patients are patients that pay at the time of service.

- Accept every form of payment possible, including American Express. I'd rather lose a couple of percentage points from my invoices than collect nothing. Take credit cards, checks, and even postdated checks. Just be sure to call the bank prior to depositing postdated checks. Also look into CareCredit, a medical credit card for patients. The company pays you, and the patient pays CareCredit. And don't forget about the payment apps like Apple Pay and Venmo. Get your money as soon as possible, however possible.

- Don't negotiate payment plans.

A viable practice keeps you, your staff, and even the patients happy.

CHAPTER 12:
Keep Your Eyes on the Prize

"Always remember, your focus determines your reality." – George Lucas

Caution: success can be very short lived. Don't let complacency set in. When things aren't going well, we usually try to figure out what's happening and what we need to do to fix it. But when things are going well, we rarely sit down to figure out what's causing our success. We get relaxed and we think things are set—that they won't change.

But things do change, and if you don't focus on your business every single day, you'll soon find yourself in a deep hole. After reading the first eleven chapters and working on your systems and protocols, you're now skilled at selling your services and collecting money, and you've built a great team that provides *WOW!* service. Now you might think that because you've done the hard work, every day will be just as good as the day before.

But one day you wake up and things are different. The systems you put in place aren't working as well as they once did, patients aren't returning for their appointments or aren't accepting your treatment recommendations, and staff are complaining and bickering. What just happened? From your perspective, you haven't changed a thing. But the truth is that you took your eyes off the prize. The reason everything was going so well before was because you paid attention to every detail in your practice. You came to work happy, smiling, and carefree. Life was good. And then it wasn't.

> The reason everything was going so well
> before was because you paid attention
> to every detail in your practice.

If you're a football fan, you may have heard of the New England Patriots head coach, Bill Belichick. Bill's facial expression never changes. He always looks grumpy, even if he's winning. I think I saw him crack a smile after he won one of his many Super Bowls. After a win, Belichick immediately goes back to the drawing board and thinks about how to win the next game. He allows his team to enjoy their success for twenty-four hours, then they refocus on the next opponent.

You're only as good as you are today. Yesterday is gone. Remember what Earl Nightingale said: "Success is the progressive realization of a worthy goal or ideal." It's a journey, not a destination. If your goal was to bring in $1 million and you've achieved that, now what? To make yesterday's $1 million, you need to make $1.2 million today.

Change is constant, and to survive and even thrive, you must adapt to it. Not too long ago, people paid the doctor, filled out an insurance form, and submitted their claims themselves. The doctor always got paid his charge, upfront, and the patient got reimbursed, but not always for the full amount. Then Medicare came about, and if the patient had this type of insurance, they would pay the doctor Medicare rates. And then someone moved the cheese. The doctor had to decide if he was going to accept insurance from a host of insurance companies or not. If he didn't, there was a good chance he'd lose volume, but if he decided to accept insurance, he'd be seeing a lot of patients at a discounted rate.

I remember when this happened to me. HMOs and PPOs came into my area of New Jersey around 2000. I had a lot of staff and my income started to decline. I read a great book that is now out of print called *Here's How Doctor* by Jon Hultman. This book and Spencer Johnson's book, *Who Moved My Cheese*, changed my life and thinking at that time. I realized that things change. It doesn't matter if you think they should or not, they just do, and you have no control over it. So, I could go to my podiatry meetings and join the bitch sessions, or I could move forward. There's no growth without change. Without change we become stale and bored. Hultman's book helped me revamp my processes.

I was making less money and I had to make some changes. I put in an EMR system, fired the medical transcriptionist, the note paster (the person who took the transcribed notes and pasted them into the patients' charts), and one medical assistant. We made appointments and discussed costs in the treatment rooms. We went virtually paperless. We were more efficient and more profitable. If I had sat around and bitched about what was happening, I'd be broke.

If you're in business, it's imperative to stay up to date on all the new technologies and equipment. Saying, "I'm sixty-five years old and am too old and tired to learn something new," or, "I'm too old to invest in new products," is a bunch of bull. If you're too old to continue to grow, then retire. Sell your practice to a young doctor. Not growing is not helping you or the community you serve. In addition, your practice will be more valuable when it's time to sell if you stay on top of everything. Further, I don't care if you're fifty, sixty, seventy, eighty, or older, you still need to grow. Growth stimulates your brain and keeps your synapses synapsing.

To prevent a sudden decline in your business, you must plan and analyze. Remember, you're a coach and you must go over the daily game plan with your team—every single day. The morning huddle with my team consists of going over the schedule and telling everyone what specifics my patients need, like X-rays, bandage changing, or suture removal. Then I tell them the focus for the day, such as, "We need to get new patients in today," or, "Remember to collect all monies the patients owe for past balances." I also use that time to review and role-play certain scenarios, or to tell the medical assistants to make sure the treatment rooms are fully stocked, or to remind the staff not to let the patients wait too long in the waiting room. It doesn't seem like you'd need to remind your staff to do these things, but you have to understand that your staff has so many things they need to accomplish during the course of the day that you need to refocus them on the key things that you want to be accomplished.

If you know your goals, you'll know where to focus. In addition to going over the schedule, every morning our marketing team reports where we stand in terms of our goals. For instance, say your monthly goal for charges is $300,000. There are twenty working days in the month, which means the practice needs to produce $15,000 a day. So, if it's the tenth working day of the month, we should be at $150,000 in charges. We tell the entire team if we're above or below that number and by how much. If we're down in charges and new patients, I tell the staff to get new patients in today. This means that when a new patient calls, we tell them that they're in luck, an appointment spot just opened up, and we can get them in today. You'll always get what you focus on, and it's your job to tell the team where their focus should lie.

Burnout

When you're young, you're so excited about your practice. It's your baby and you love feeding it and watching it grow. Then, sometime in your forties, you start thinking there's something more for you out there. You wonder why you aren't further ahead in your life. You work hard, but you're tired. You wake up in the morning and hit the snooze button four to five times before moseying around and getting in the shower. You're no longer energized to go to work. This is *burnout*.

However, you may not realize you're suffering from burnout. Instead, you may think that you don't like being a podiatrist anymore. You want to work less and make more money, and you can't see yourself doing this job for another twenty or thirty years.

Then you get distracted. One day you get a call from one of your friends who wants to talk about this amazing product that makes people look and feel younger. She tells you how she'd suffered from severe knee pain and went to her orthopedist, who recommended surgery. Instead, she applied this cream and now, at age forty-five, she can do 180s in a half pipe without any pain. And, by the way, this is also a great business opportunity. Now you're intrigued—maybe there is something better out there.

I've dabbled in a couple of outside endeavors myself. I've made some money doing them, but my practice suffered. You see, I've spent most of my life learning how to become the best podiatrist possible and to run a professional practice. This is my expertise. I just needed to figure out how to make it fun again. Some wise person once told me, "Do what you know and continue to get better at it."

I learned that a practice can be comprised of several mini-practices. There are so many little businesses inside your practice. You can add physical therapy, prosthetics, a shoe store, a spa, and a pain management system—even a neuropathy clinic. Or you could specialize in pediatrics or sports medicine. There are endless ideas out there to make you more money with less stress while having fun. But you won't continue to grow if your mind is totally stressed out. Stress closes your brain to new ideas.

Why does the burnout syndrome usually happen in your forties? When you started your career, your life may have been a lot simpler. But now you have a significant other, children, a house, and a lot of other responsibilities that you didn't have before. Your attention is needed in so many places. This leads to feeling overwhelmed, which can lead to anxiety or depression. Feeling overwhelmed and anxious comes from lack of clarity, which means that you don't really know what you want, or you don't know what's really important to you.

We're all service providers. We're educators and servants. We do what we do because we love helping people. And we help people who are in pain, which means they aren't always the nicest or easiest to get along with. If you take things personally, then I'm afraid you won't live a happy life. Learn to do your best and that doing your best is all you can do. You can't help everyone, so focus on the people you can help and guide the ones you can't.

Learn to do your best and that doing your best is all you can do. You can't help everyone, so focus on the people you can help and guide the ones you can't.

Learn what's really important in your life. What are the things you truly can't live without? The answer is simple. It starts with *you*. You can't live without yourself, so get some good sleep, drink lots of water, eat right, exercise, and meditate to gain peace of mind. Then focus on your significant other and family. Make sure you have time every week to do something you love. It could be as simple as going to the movies or having a nice dinner. Put your phone away, and focus on the life and people around you.

Remember the phrase, "If you want something done, ask a busy person"? Busy people get things done because they plan for it. Michael Hyatt said, "What gets scheduled, gets done." Plan your day and week. Stephen Covey talked about working on the big rocks first. These rocks aren't your business. Instead, they're the things that truly matter, like exercise and meditation. Put your family time in and don't forget the fun time. Then put in your rainmaker day and plan what you're going to work on that day. Your rainmaker day is the day you do not see patients, but you simply work on your business, and it won't happen if it isn't planned. Other things will consume the time, and you could end up using it to run errands or go to the dentist.

Think about the areas of your practice you need to bolster. Is it marketing and finances? If so, use that day to meet with your marketing and financial directors or your bookkeeper. Maybe you'll use the time to write your blogs or shoot videos. Your rainmaker day is also a good time to review your processes. Walk around the office and see if there are any bottlenecks. Can you think of ways to streamline every system in your practice? Take notes. Don't interrupt your staff to discuss these things during their workday. One more thing—on this day, you shouldn't be disturbed by your staff. Put a "do not disturb" note on your door. Don't answer emails or messages unless it's a true emergency. This allows you to focus on your plan, plus it teaches your staff to make decisions without you.

One more warning: beware of the shiny object syndrome. As of this writing, the average person sees around 4,000 to 10,000 advertisements on social media per day. That's right. *Per day*. And, of course, the ads are directed at what you like, based upon what you've viewed and searched. You might be compelled to get sucked in by something that distracts you away from your primary source of income—your podiatry practice. Or you might hear about a newfangled machine that doctors are using to bring in loads of cash. There's no harm in listening to these ideas, but then conduct your due diligence.

When I hear about something new that sounds like it could be helpful to my practice, I immediately do my research. A perfect example of this is when extracorporeal shock wave therapy came about. I met Dr. David

Zuckerman at a conference, and he was really excited about this technology. I was skeptical but also intrigued. I drove ninety minutes to his office to see him treat a patient. This was high-energy ESWT with the Dornier machine. I met several patients and interviewed them. The patients paid $2,500 for the procedure. One patient said he'd had the procedure done on his other foot the month before and was now pain free. The technology met my criteria in that it couldn't cause any harm, and I had patients who needed this procedure. Plus, I didn't have to buy the machine. Dr. Zuckerman drove the machine to my office. The cost of the procedure was never a factor. If there's a need and it works and it helps my patients avoid surgery, then to me it's a no-brainer.

Opportunities will keep coming your way as long as your mind is open—meaning you're not overly stressed—so keep your ears open and do your research immediately. Then make a decision quickly. Don't wait. Slow decision-making costs you money and creates stress.

If you apply the information given in this book, your chance of burnout will be slim.

If you apply the information given in this book, your chance of burnout will be slim. You'll learn to become a great leader and to help your staff become great leaders. Establishing repeatable processes is critical to success. Hiring key people, training and re-training your staff, and allowing them to make key decisions will remove a lot from your plate. When you add in a rainmaker day your practice will be fun again.

Keeping your eyes on the prize—your practice—doesn't mean you need to hyper-focus on it 24/7. The goal is to not be stressed out. Take the time at night or early the next morning to reflect on the day. Write the answers to these questions in a journal:

- What went right?
- What could be better?
- What are you truly grateful for?

When you write down the answers, you're actually doing a brain dump—clearing your mind and creating a new path for you to grow.

You became a podiatrist to help people. This, doctor, is your super-power. Keep that power energized on a daily basis!

I want to end the book with a quote from Peter F. Drucker. "Follow effective action with quiet reflection. From the quiet reflection will come even more effective action."

Acknowledgments

My first word of appreciation goes to my amazing girlfriend, Jaimie. I met Jaimie by swiping right on Tinder, and it was the best move I ever made. Jaimie knew of my desire to write a book and was extremely supportive. Thank you for believing in me and giving me confidence, not only in writing this book, but in any endeavor I seek. I love you very much.

Next, I thank Rem Jackson, owner of Top Practices. I met Rem at his very first summit meeting about eleven years ago. We were introduced by a mutual friend, Mike Crosby. Mike said, "You have to go to Rem's meeting about goal setting." I said, "Goal setting? I've been setting goals since high school." Mike told me that I should at least speak to Rem. So, I called and Rem convinced me to go to his meeting. He said that if I didn't get something out of it, he'd refund my money. I'm so glad I decided to go. No matter how much you think you know about a subject, you can always learn more. I definitely learned a lot that day, but the best thing that came out of that meeting was my long friendship and business partnership with Rem. He has been a friend, a coach, a mentor, and a business partner. We started the Virtual Practice Management Institute along with Tina Del Buono, and because of our relationship, we've been able to help many podiatrists with their practices.

Rem introduced me to Nancy Erickson, owner of The Book Professor. Nancy was my book coach for this book, in addition to being my editor and publisher. Nancy is so easy to work with, and she made writing this book an extremely delightful experience. She was very encouraging during the process, and I even had the chance to meet her in person at one of Rem's summit meetings. Nancy will tell you that everyone has a book in them, and if you've ever thought about writing a book, contact her at www.thebookprofessor.com. I always wanted to write my own book but didn't think it was the right time to do so. Nancy customized a plan that worked specifically for me, and without her, this book would never have been written. You may think you don't have the time to write a book now, but like bunion surgery, there's never a good time to do it. So, just do it.

I want to thank my sister, Debbie, and my brother-in-law, Jeff. I have a very small family, and I'm grateful for their love and support. No matter what I dream about doing, they always support me and believe in me. Love you guys.

I love every aspect of practicing podiatry, both the medicine and the business sides. Along the way of learning how to become a better business-person—and simply a better person overall—I met three amazing guys. The first is Tom Foster. I met Tom at one of Rem's conferences. Tom is the owner of Foster Web Marketing. To me, they're the best at providing great websites and SEO. Tom is more than a business associate; he's a true friend. He has been with me in good and rough times, and I know if I ever need anything, Tom will be there.

Next, I thank Dave Frees. Dave is a lawyer, but I won't hold that against him! Dave is simply the smartest man I've ever come across. He is known as the Master of Communication and teaches courses on that subject and persuasion. He also authored a book called *The Language of Parenting: Building Great Family Relationships At All Ages*. Once, I drove over two and a half hours with my son, Sam, to see Dave. Dave took time out of his really crazy schedule to speak with Sam to help him get through a tough time. I'll never forget that. Dave puts on an annual event called Business Black Ops, where he teaches marketing, communication, and persuasion. A lot of my practice success is attributed to Dave's teachings.

Then there's Jay Henderson, the owner of Real Talent Hiring. In chapter 4, I talk about how Jay can help you make sure you're surrounded by the right type of people who will help you grow your business. Like Dave Frees and Tom Foster, Jay is more than someone I do business with. Jay is a man of action, and I have a deep admiration for him.

I'm very grateful for my team at Family Foot & Ankle Specialists. They've been with me throughout this journey, and I'm blessed to have an amazing staff, which I consider my family away from regular family. Specifically, I want to thank Jessica Taveras, my marketing and public relations director. She and my administrator, Sarah Avilleira, have helped me with certain aspects of this book. They are extremely talented and made the job of writing this book a lot easier. I also want to thank Andrea Mathews, who's ridden the roller coaster of my life with me. Thanks for being a great financial administrator, friend, and listener.

I always say that coaches need coaches. So, I want to thank my Anthony Robbins' coach, Cathy Hanlin. Cathy is simply fantastic. She's so uplifting and has kept me on target to get this book, plus my other goals, accomplished. Never do anything alone. If you want to get something done, get a coach.

In 2019, I became a member of the Legacy Builders Mastermind. As you can see, I don't rely only on podiatry meetings and groups to gain knowledge. There are so many different people and organizations to surround yourself with in order to be the best you can be. Legacy Builders helps me achieve my goals outside of podiatry. One of them is to become a great motivational leader and business coach. I want to thank Bryan Dulaney, Nick Unsworth, and Casey Thornton for their help and support.

Then there is my practice coach, Vidya Sartorius. I have known Vidya for years, and whenever I have a problem in my practice, I turn to her. Like I've said before, sometimes you need a fresh pair of eyes to see what's going on in your practice because you can't see what's right in front of you. Thanks, Vidya, for being there when I need you.

To all the members of Top Performers, past and present, thank you for your opinions and advice. Top Performers is the mastermind built within Rem Jackson's Top Practices group. This is an elite group of people who get together three times a year to help solve each other's problems and discuss what's working for us. During one of our masterminds, I met an Australian podiatrist, Tyson Franklin. Tyson is simply amazing. He has two podcasts and has written a few books. He's an inspiration, and I've learned so much from this Aussie.

Writing a book is more than just sitting down and putting words to paper. You need to be in the right mindset, and, for me, exercise plays a major role in doing so. For this, I want to thank my personnel trainer, Aviv Wagner. I am a big believer in the mind-body connection. Thanks, Aviv, for keeping me in shape.

Thanks also to Tina Del Buono, my coaching partner at the Virtual Practice Management Institute. I love being around Tina because she's an extremely positive person. Tina never sees problems; she sees solutions and new ways of doing things. We both share a passion for personal development, and you can find us often drinking a glass of wine and discussing our latest readings from leaders like Brendon Burchard, John Maxwell, Anthony Robbins, and Dean Graziosi, to name a few. Tina is a delight to work with and she's excellent at what she does.

I mentioned them in the Introduction, but I must again thank Doctors Irvin Donick and Bruce Werber, as well as Dr. Paul Scherer. Dr. Scherer accepted me as the Fellow at Hadassah University Medical Center and was the master at teaching biomechanics. He touched so many people and I still think about him. May he rest in peace.

There are so many people for whom I'm grateful, and I want to thank all the teachers I've had in my life. Never underestimate a good teacher. That being said, my last thank goes to Dr. Edwin Wolf, who was my mentor during my first year in residency. I learned a lot from him, and I am ever so grateful.

About the Author

Dr. Peter Wishnie has practiced podiatry in central New Jersey for over thirty years. He completed his undergraduate studies at Stony Brook University in Long Island, New York, then studied podiatric medicine at the California College of Podiatric Medicine (now called The California School of Podiatric Medicine at Samuel Merritt University). After a one-year surgical residency at Parson's Hospital in Queens, New York, he received a fellowship in foot and ankle surgery at Hadassah Hospital in Jerusalem, Israel.

In 1989, Dr. Wishnie purchased a practice in Piscataway, New Jersey. Since then he's opened a second practice in Hillsborough, New Jersey and has three associates. He's a student of personal development and is a John Maxwell certified leadership coach. Dr. Wishnie is the Director of Physician Programming at Top Practices, an organization that helps podiatrists to market and manage their practices.

Dr. Wishnie is board certified by the American Board of Podiatric Surgery and is a fellow of the American Academy of Podiatric Practice Management. He has lectured on many different topics of practice management both nationally and internationally. He has three sons, Samuel, Alec, and Benjamin, and an amazing girlfriend, Jaimie. He enjoys all sports, especially baseball and football. He's an avid concert goer and enjoys going to the gym. He lives in Somerville, New Jersey.

Join the Top Practices Virtual Practice Management Institute

The Top Practices Virtual Practice Management Institute (VPMI), led by Dr. Peter Wishnie and Tina Del Buono, is a breakthrough concept in practice management coaching, training, and support. Members of the VPMI have 24/7 access to a treasure trove of resources online, covering every issue and challenge medical practices face. Answers, documents, systems, and protocols combined with direct instruction from Dr. Wishnie and Ms. Del Buono provide the most in-depth, comprehensive, and affordable program available anywhere. Members work with our coaches on their action plans as they improve their practices in a step-by-step program. Get your nights and weekends back by managing your practice like a pro.

Visit www.TopPractices.com/Prosperity to learn more about this breakthrough approach to outstanding practice management. If you're ready, your practice can be a dream rather than a nightmare. Please join us!

How You Can Work Directly with Dr. Wishnie

In addition to the extensive online resources and courses of The Virtual Practice Management Institute, Dr. Wishnie works directly with a limited number of coaching clients in the following ways:

- Individual coaching programs. One-on-one intensive coaching with Dr. Wishnie to achieve and exceed your specific goals. This first requires an in-depth interview with Dr. Wishnie and acceptance into the program. To arrange the interview and learn how the program works, email Peter@TopPractices.com.

- Specialized in-person training in small groups. Find out more about these programs and the schedule at www.TopPractices.com/Prosperity.

- Seminars on leadership, protocols, management, finances of medical practices, and more. Go to www.TopPractices.com/Prosperity for more information and dates.